19.99

Sacred Book of Earth

Pantheon of Aeternam

authorHOUSE®

AuthorHouse™ UK
1663 Liberty Drive
Bloomington, IN 47403 USA
www.authorhouse.co.uk
Phone: UK TFN: 0800 0148641 (Toll Free inside the UK)
        UK Local: 02036 956322 (+44 20 3695 6322 from outside the UK)

Published by AuthorHouse 01/07/2021

ISBN: 978-1-6655-8408-1 (sc)
ISBN: 978-1-6655-8409-8 (e)

PANTHEON OF AETERNAM

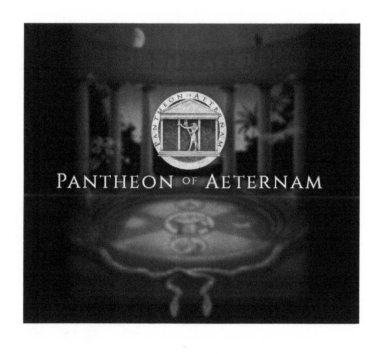

PANTHEON OF AETERNAM

GOD THOTH

PANTHEON of AETERNAM

Barbara
MESSENGER

PANTHEON OF AETERNAM

Robbert-jan Rozenkruis

PANTHEON OF AETERNAM

CONTENTS

Acknowledgement

We would like to express the deepest gratitude to all our order members, friends, and supporters of our work who have helped us spread the teachings of the gods and bring light to Earth. Furthermore, we would like to thank the readers of this book and all of you who continue to support our work. We are confident that the "Sacred Book of Earth" will be a catalyst of truth regarding Earth's creation and her purpose as a Creator God and open the way to all of you who seek truth to connect to Earth's creative power and grow in unity.

PREFACE

We are very proud to present this book to you as it is the most powerful and truthful account of Earth's creation and sets the starting point for humanity to journey back to Earth of the golden era, experience her powerful creative powers, gifts, purpose, path and bring this high point of growth in their present moment. The cosmic wisdom that is shared in this book will take you to a time where physicality did not exist. The only plane where all life was created, was the astral plane.

The astral plane is a complex electromagnetic field and its energy occupies the greatest part of the cosmic creation. It is an enormous, multidimensional energy space of transformation which is divided into many sub-planes of various energetic structures. It is the home of our astral body which is our permanent and eternal existence. There was a time that all beings including Earth, experienced life only in the astral plane. The creation of physicality was a transformation of the astral body that was allowed to be experienced by a small number of astral beings. It was seen as a unique creation, leading to an extension of the astral plane.

The astral beings that chose to experience this unique transformation, became the planets that were called to form star systems and create life themselves, connecting to the gods and the Light of the Source. Earth was a high receiver and transmitter of light. She supported her transformation and growth cycles by receiving and transmitting cosmic light and becoming a high creator. When she completed her transformation, becoming the physical planet, she went through a growth cycle that is called the golden era.

In the golden era, Earth carried the highest light; her physicality and astral existence were fully connected and carried the same light. Her creation, animals, plants, and other living beings were part of the same unity, existing in the same light. There were no polarities, distortion, fear, or limitation on Earth during the golden era, only constant growth.

Earth remained in a high state of growth even when other planets and their creation had started to experience distortion and schisms. Earth supported the growth of all living beings in this new physical plane, by sharing light, supporting and building energy fields, allowing the cosmic light to connect and support life.

This book will show you how and why Earth's golden era came to an end. You will read about the transformations that Earth and other planets had to experience during these turbulent times and how this affected their creation.

This book offers invaluable cosmic wisdom including teachings communicated to the messengers of Pantheon of Aeternam, Barbara, and Robbert-jan Rozenkruis by the Light of Thoth. They have been instructed by the Thoth to receive these unique teachings and make them available to everyone who is an open channel and wants to connect to truth and cosmic wisdom. There is no secret knowledge to be kept for the selected few. All wisdom is revealed to all who are interested in becoming truth. We do not teach dogma, philosophy, or other man-made theory. We teach ageless wisdom and cosmic truth is given to us by the High Gods of the pleroma.

They want to inform people about the creation of planet Earth, the full story of her growth and transformation which was hidden for thousands of years. The teachings of the gods will help humanity reconnect to the Earth's energies, be part of the planet's growth, and live in harmony with all species. We all have to support Earth and restore her to the most graceful expression of herself, her golden age. We are all connected to the Earth of the golden era; this is our starting point where all questions can be answered and all wisdom is shared to assist evolution. We are all connected to Earth's growth and rebirth and this is the journey that is offered to the readers of this book.

The process of communication between the gods and the messengers cannot be explained or described; it is a cosmic process that is supported by Earth and cosmic energies. They received this gift in order to assist the gods to communicate and awake humanity during this crucial time in Earth's history. The messengers don't try to explain the communication process; they are very grateful that they were chosen and have made this work the focus of their lives.

The teachings presented in this book have not been altered or edited. They are faithful accounts of the wisdom of the gods.

For more information about the Pantheon of Aeternam you can visit our website.

http://pantheonofaeternam.com

The order Pantheon of Aeternam is open to all. There is no secret knowledge to be kept for the selected few; instead, all wisdom should be revealed to all who are interested in becoming truth. This is an important time and we all have to support Earth and restore her to the most graceful expression of herself, her golden age. There is a divine plan and a high project of creation that involves humanity and Earth experiencing cosmic growth. Thoth's teachings are spreading to Earth in order to restore truth, high light, and bring growth for all human beings and their mother Earth. Humanity and Earth are called to connect and follow the divine plan and common purpose. The order Pantheon of Aeternam is open to all. There is no secret knowledge to be kept for the selected few; instead, all wisdom should be revealed to all who are interested in becoming truth. This is an important time and we all have to support Earth and restore her to the most graceful expression of herself, her golden age.

What is the Pantheon of Aeternam?

In 2014, Barbara and Robbert-jan Rozenkruis created the order Pantheon of Aeternam. Their unity has supported their project and offered great healing to both of them and thousands of people who connect to their work.

The moment they met, they became aware of their common purpose. Robbert-jan and Barbara are very different, come from different experiences and backgrounds, lived in different countries but they share a common path. The light that they shared created a new life for both of them and a common purpose. When they first met they started having communication with Christian Rosencreutz. The messages they received guided them to overcome different obstacles and start building their life together. They received teachings and guidance that helped them heal, connect to their whole being, and open up to the cosmic light of Thoth.

Their process of communication with Thoth cannot be explained or described; it is a cosmic process that supports their unity with all life. They do not perform any rituals, they are not restricted to have this communication only on certain times/days at a special location or at a specific high energy spot. They do not use crystals, sounds, symbols, or plant medicine. They are a pure channel of Thoth's energy and the connection is instant, direct, and can take place any time, whenever they want to offer healing and light to Earth and humanity.

They have received thousands of teachings, some of them are published in their books "Fountain Source of High Wisdom-Sacred Book of Thoth", "Wisdom of Thoth", Sacred Book of Earth, and many others they share with members of their community for healing purposes and cosmic expansion. The purpose of this gift is to awaken humanity to their true power to grow with Earth and prepare them for a new phase of growth. They are very grateful that they were chosen to carry this gift and they have made this work the focus of their lives.

When they first started to communicate with the Light of Thoth they had profound experiences that led to an awakening. The Light created a sacred place in them, an expansive energy field, and then connected to their own light, initiating purification from all limitations and connection to their true-self. When you connect to your true self, your life becomes an open path of limitless growth and transformation. This is how you can become the creator of your own life and purify your whole being from the distortion that exists on Earth. The light of the cosmos is a great guide, healer, transformer, and creator, supporting humanity and Earth to find their way back to the Golden Age.

Human beings and Earth have a collective purpose and are able to receive the light and grow in unity. The physical body is created by Earth who is aware of our purpose and divine plan. In other words, we are all here as a gift to Earth, supporting Earth's growth. We exist in unity with Earth and her creation and this is how we grow.

Thoth's teachings are cosmic wisdom and teach humanity about cosmic laws, Earth's creation and purpose, enlightenment, healing, distortion on Earth, reincarnation, the astral plane, the pleroma, and much more.

Barbara and Robbert-jan had established a constant connection with the Light of Thoth and received hundreds of teachings and guidance. The time came when they were instructed by Thoth to create the Pantheon of Aeternam as a gift to humanity. All the teachings they received, should be shared with all people who chose growth and creation as their path. It is important that we all become perfect receivers and transmitters of light, we all grow together, exist in unity, and be part of the divine plan.

Robert-jan and Barbara want to teach humanity a life of unity and effortless growth and the teachings that they share will help people purify from all imbalances, connect to their own being, experience their path, and exist in unity with Earth and the cosmos. Their high duty is to connect humanity with Earth and the cosmos; clear all illusion and distortion and restore the high vibrational LIGHT that once existed on Earth during the golden era.

Human beings are coming to Earth having a purpose and a divine plan, unique abilities leading to an effortless life of receiving and transmitting LIGHT, growth, and transformation. The truth in you is not a belief or an idea; it is a living being that can connect you with Earth and her high light that is her golden era as well as the infinite cosmic growth.

When you connect to your true self, you understand the divine plan and purpose of your reincarnation, your abilities to grow, and your unique way to connect to others and support their growth.

When human beings understand and experience these connections they will enter a greater space of growth. Limitations/fears/separation can affect the mind and the physical body when a being is confused, disconnected from truth, and unaware of their purpose in this lifetime. When human beings are in this state they are powerless against distortion. Life on Earth becomes a traumatic experience and the mind focuses on the pain. Human beings have the ability to share, connect, and grow with others; if your mind is affected by distortion you can only spread distortion. People should experience freedom. You are free to love yourself and connect to Earthly and cosmic nourishment, experience healing, transformation, and growth. There are many gifts that are stored in you: your light, truth, pure intention can help you experience freedom. You are free to connect to Earth and nourish yourselves, heal, and grow.

The Pantheon of Aeternam was created to accomplish a special duty: to purify humanity and create the coming of a new golden era on Earth. With Thoth's teachings, they want to restore truth and freedom and bring high growth to all human beings and their mother Earth. Human beings need to purify from distortion that breeds illusion, artificiality, and fragmentation. We have to learn to exist in a space of unity; act with purity and focus on growth. Disconnect from illusionary thoughts, expectations, and ideals allow healing to enter your being. This can be achieved when people go through a process of purification and transformation.

Purification is an exercise of knowing, healing, and empowerment and you should follow it. Look at your imbalances with acceptance. Learn to be an observer of your own actions and be aware of their impact. Connect to your being, quieten your mind, disconnect from the persona. Truth is your only tool to high wisdom. In this space of truth, you are called to purify yourself and allow healing to reach your imbalances. Open to the light of the cosmos that can heal you and nourish you. Your connection to the light will purify and bring balance to you. By connecting to the cosmic light, knowing yourself, and having pure intention, you are transforming and moving closer to your higher self.

Purification is a unique self-healing process and includes the study and practice of observation, creating a space of peace, connecting to your whole being, and allowing the energies of the cosmos and Earth to enter your body and start your healing process. When people practice purification they experience intense healing that purifies them from imbalances, trauma, and fear patterns. Life can become an effortless flow of growth when people are free to follow their path.

Pantheon of Aeternam has published two more books that can be used as a guide to help you discover cosmic truths shared by Thoth and start your healing process.

The first book "Fountain Source of High Wisdom-Sacred Book of Thoth" was published in February 2015. In this book, there are more than 200 teachings, a complete vocabulary section plus extra teaching material including more than forty questions and answers. The teachings in this book share light on many topics including the creation of Earth, Earth races, Cosmic creation, Astral plane, Higher self, Creation code, Reincarnation, Cosmic laws, Growth, Purpose, Cosmic Healing, Love, Manipulation on Earth, Living the illusion,

Transformation of a physical being, The Connection between Physical and Astral Body, True Seekers of Wisdom in Ancient Times, Hollow of the Earth, Conscious Living and the ideal State of Humanity. For more information about our book, you can visit our website: http://pantheonofaeternam.co.uk/fountain-source-of-high-wisdom-sacred-book-of-tho th.html

Pantheon of Aeternam's second book has the title "Wisdom of Thoth" and was published in February 2019. This book was created to help you connect to truth and express it in your everyday life and creative process. It contains more than 300 pages of cosmic wisdom and focuses on Healing, Purification, Connecting to Earth's energies, Growth, Dealing with imbalances, Observing patterns, Illusion-Fear-Limitation, Building communities of truth, and many more. Read more about this book on the Pantheon of Aeternam's website: http://pantheonofaeternam.co.uk/books.html#wisdomofthoth

CHAPTER I

We all exist in unity and growth. This is our driving force to help us connect to the Source. When you understand that all beings are created to experience unity by receiving and transmitting light then you will experience the cosmos being part of yourself. We are all connected to each other and energy, which is information, passes from one body to another. If you have the skill to translate the cosmic information and bring it to your own plane then you are a creator.

What are you creating on Earth?

Human beings will need to create communities that support freedom, truth, and growth. All people united will connect to their purpose and develop new skills in transmitting and receiving energy. Earth supports healthy communities that are able to grow following the natural laws. Earth wants to be involved in our communities, she wants to offer her light but she also wants us to generate light and feed the whole planet. These are the natural laws and Earth was created to fulfill her purpose of a god-creator- planet, supporting the light of her beings.

Creating communities of truth and growth is the ultimate goal. The more human beings are able to connect to the truth the more clarity will receive, regarding their purpose, connecting to Earth and building communities that will heal the schisms and bring growth. We need communities where people are supported in their evolution, developing their skills, studying true methods, and fulfilling their purpose. With our whole existence, we support and complement each other inventing new ways of transmitting and receiving energy.

There is a miraculous way of living and this is being detached from beliefs, dogmas, and archetypal behavior. All the above have been created to help you focus and sustain a certain consciousness and life experience. We are asking you now to abandon and destroy the persona and the lifestyle. Our aim is to give everybody the tools they need in order to paint their own authentic picture of themselves and let their true purpose be revealed. We want you to detach yourself from all that you are, right now and connect to your true self, the one that is known to the masters and gods.

When you are connected to life you will wake up and look for truth which is a great tool for growth. Human beings are not aware that behind closed doors there are beings that are planning total destruction and they are convinced that the downfall of Earth is evolution. You are not going to make the plans reality by walking the path they have created for you. You must know that at the end of this path is the destruction of the human race. We are calling you now and we are asking you to disconnect from all artificialities. Your true-self is precious and has the high light you seek; this is the only path for evolution.

In an ideal community, people should not have to deal with schedules, diaries, daily tasks and appointment lists. In an ideal society, you should be allowed to work the times that you are fully productive and have time to go through your own process of transformation and growth. When you undertake any type of work you should be prepared and well equipped to do it to a high standard.

An expression of distortion on planet Earth is when people are forced to perform certain tasks without support or preparation time. This leads to poor performance which will affect the lives and work of all people connected to this one person. I also see on Earth that poor performance is the norm; perfection is unknown because people are behaving like surviving slaves.

I want you to look at yourselves and observe the patterns I already mentioned in your life and the life of others. Are you in the right state to be perfect in what you do and be part of perfection? Do you understand perfection and how it is linked to your everyday life and work? Can you see what is blocking you from escaping the survival mode and entering the creator state? What is the impact of your lifestyle on you and the people close to you?

When you are behaving like slaves, you are losing your humanity; the only way to freedom is through your truth. There are many ways used to convince you that you have to remain a slave although the truth about your current state is never mentioned to you: You have to remain a slave for your family, for social and financial success, to attract others, to follow what others do.

They are people who think that being a slave will bring them freedom and happiness and they fully surrender to the illusion. The result of all this is an imbalanced life full of disease, confusion and dissatisfaction. You are diseased if you allow yourself to become a slave when your true nature and purpose is to be free and connect to cosmic laws. You can go against the plan of slavery any time you wish. You just have to wake up to the understanding that most people's lives are formed by a contagious disease called illusion. You have the power to escape, remember that illusion has no life or true power over you. Now is the time that people on Earth take responsibility for their lives and wake up to a new and meaningful existence. If you are seeking enlightenment, the illusion is your first challenge.

Introduction

Illusion can take many forms and can capture the people that are looking for truth. To avoid this and truly disconnect from all artificiality you have to look in yourself, your connection with Earth.

Connecting to Earth will help you understand your true purpose and how to connect to your physical body, energy growth and high light. Your purpose is a life of truth, higher consciousness and supporting others to rediscover their true-self. If you wish to be a creator that is the path you have to take.

Wisdom of Thoth: Why is it important to connect to Earth

Human beings are encouraged to believe in theories and not to experience their own life on Earth. Your religions and experts in mythology, history, science and spirituality want you to believe in their theories but none of them encourages you to connect to Earth and experience her powerful creative force. When you connect to Earth you become aware of your purpose and you use your physical body to receive and transmit light in order to balance Earth's energies.

When you connect to information and see it as an opportunity to enter the social pyramid and climb up to the top, the power that you seek becomes your limitation. When you connect to Earth, you are able to understand your purpose and experience it in your everyday life; you understand your unique abilities and you use them to fulfill your purpose, experience unity with everything that exists and understand that your growth is part of the cosmic growth.

If you are not able to understand Earth's growth and connect to her golden era it is because you are not able to connect to her light and do not allow her to nourish you and help you develop your abilities. When you connect to Earth you will be able to experience her golden era and make it a reality for all her creation.

Introduction

Can you describe your space of truth? What does it consist of and what is your contribution to keep it alive? How can you unite with other beings in this space and make it expand? Human beings have to make decisions about their own lives and be creators of their own growth. Information on Earth is often a diversion from the truth or keeping the mind in a fantasy world while the rest of your being is following the illusion.

I do not want you to see this teaching as information but as a guide to help you act and move out of the maze of illusion and into a space of truth. Connecting to the cosmic light and purifying yourself are gifts you can give to others and together you can co-create this space of truth. Healing and unity are necessary for humanity and Earth's growth. Connect to your pure intention and you will be able to connect to your whole being and then to humanity and Earth.

Wisdom of Thoth: Earth's Divine Plan

When one looks at the ocean, he is not able to see every single drop that exists in unity with countless other drops. You cannot distinguish one drop from the other because now they exist to form this ocean and allow the current to create the movement necessary for this creation. When human beings are able to see themselves as part of Earth's creation and be in constant unity with her then fragmentation, division and distortion on the planet will evaporate. When you see yourself as part of Earth's creation, you will not experience hunger or pain because Earth can nourish you and support your ability to become a perfect receiver and transmitter of light.

If all humanity understands and opens up to Earth's energies then you all will be able to heal yourselves and transform your physical body. If humanity can heal distortion and fragmentation then Earth will remember her golden era and she will produce the right nourishment and high energies to help you transform into the high being of the golden era. This will happen when humanity exists in unity and this state experiences a deep healing and purification process. The next step is to recognize its purpose to become Earth's receivers and transmitters. When each individual is able to connect to Earth and receive her energy, all her creation will go on a process of purification and experience unity. This is Earth's divine plan.

Introduction

All elements are connected to Earth and this is why they stay connected to you. If our Source has created Earth then your connection with our Source is direct and without boundaries. The only boundaries that block your way are the ones created by illusion and accepted by you.

If you were able to connect to Earth she could show you the connections between the elements, the creation being an extension of the cosmos and the cosmic light. The cosmic light is the essence of the cosmos. It is the seed of our Source that is planted in all beings and in all planes. Your being is created by this seed and becomes a womb to carry the seed for a new creation.

Life is growth and this is experienced in all planes. Earth will tell you this when you are able to connect to her and will show you that birth never stops and has no end. This is how you should see your lives; constantly growing, transforming, becoming the womb for the cosmic light to create and then experience growth around you. If you ignore this cosmic law then you exist in illusion and you are responsible for blocking your own growth and connection to the Source.

Wisdom of Thoth: How can we connect to Earth?

Many people want to connect to Earth, receive her healing, and be part of her purpose and growth but many of their thoughts and actions become an obstacle and turn them against this connection. The mind will explain the process of connection with Earth as an impossible task. Questions and thoughts will become diversions: I do not know how; I do not have time; I need to focus on some important issues now; others do not appreciate my ability to connect to Earth so it will not make me popular; connecting to Earth is not an important skill for growth and advancement.

The mind can create all these and many more distractions to pull you away from your path and purpose: connecting to Earth is your purpose. Some of you may ask how can I achieve this if I am distracted by everyday patterns that although seem to be important, are diversions from my truth and purpose. You can connect to Earth if you are able to connect to your whole being and understand that your life form is an extension of Earth's life form. For this to happen you have to dive into the greatness of your being. Loving yourself and healing yourself are qualities that you are going to develop when you are connected to your being.

When you make this your everyday experience, you will be able to observe your connection with Earth. You can energetically communicate with Earth wherever you are and this can be achieved when you connect to your own being and see yourself as an open space of countless opportunities for growth. Your physical body can be healed when it is connected to Earth's physical body. When you live close to Nature, observing Earth's cycles of growth, plant seeds, and nourish your physical body with Earth's creative force will help you to purify your life from everyday tasks and patterns that take you on a diversion and align your whole being with Earth's growth.

Introduction

All beings that have reincarnated on Earth are connecting to her energies and bring light to her being. Remember that the human state that you are experiencing right now is not permanent; you are astral beings who are in constant evolution and will never be controlled by anything and anybody other than the cosmic laws. When human beings are fully awake then they will connect to their true purpose and will

allow the high energies to heal Earth. All creation is united to a common goal and this will bring awakening to planet Earth.

Wisdom of Thoth: What is the source?

The light in all beings is expanding in order to move to higher planes and finally connect to the Source. This is how creation grows and regenerates itself. All beings have a natural ability to grow to higher planes and the energy fields and grids support this growth. There is a constant communication within your being, between you and your astral body, higher self, and creation code.

This communication can be seen as an energy exchange and creates countless opportunities for growth, guiding you on your path. All beings want to connect to the source because they want to renew the starting point of their creation. This can only happen when you connect to your creator and reestablish and energetic communication.

Some of you may ask what is the Source? The source is the highest creator light and all cosmic life is sitting on the light of the source. The same way that Earth is supporting her creation. Allowing growth and nourishment to enter her creation, the source creates in a similar way and everything that creates is part of its light. There is no separation between beings that exist in different planes and the source. Some of you want to ask what created the source?

The light beings that exist in the astral plane have no beginning or end; they have unlimited opportunities for growth. They can receive and transmit constantly. This constant movement of light that brings life to all beings is the essence of the source. The source is in constant movement, regeneration, and growth and this is why the qualities of its life are constantly being renewed and its existence and ability to create has no beginning or end. People can describe the source as self-created but there is another form of life that is supporting the creation of the source.

Introduction

The human beings that exist on the surface of the planet are not able to enter the hollow Earth and experience life there. This is caused by the difference in vibration and the types of growth. Signs of the golden age are still apparent in the inner parts of the planet and affect their growth. All beings who exist there are able to connect to high energies; this allows Earth to continue being a creator.

Wisdom of Thoth: Life in the inner core of the Earth

Earth's physical body was created to have a high vibration similar to her astral body in the astral plane. She is a high creator who has the ability to receive high light and guide her creation to high growth. Earth's creative abilities and high growth can be experienced by the beings that exist in the inner Earth. They have their own civilizations that were created when Earth started to experience low vibrational beings entering her atmospheres.

The beings that exist in the inner Earth are experiencing the golden era. Their body, abilities, path, and purpose are very different from the human beings that currently exist on the surface of the Earth. These beings carry with them the light of the golden era and have made their home in the inner Earth. This is a great opportunity for them because they connect to Earth's high energies and this shapes their life and purpose.

You may want to ask: do these beings wish to come to the surface of the Earth and are they able to? Human beings have the illusion that alien visitors want to invade their lands and interfere in their lives. You must know that the surface of the Earth is the low vibrational part of the planet and if any planetary visitors wanted to visit Earth they would prefer to enter the inner core.

You also have to know that the idea of a spaceship landing on a field or hovering above one of your cities can only exist in your fantasy. Planetary visitors can travel to other planes energetically. Their energy is a point of connection and a powerful transformation tool to help them achieve what is important for their growth and the growth of their planet or plane.

The beings who exist in the inner Earth are fully aware of their path and Earth's path. They are able to see what is happening in all parts of Earth and they are also able to connect to other astral beings and communicate with them. Your purpose is to get out of your confusion, connect to Earth, and focus on your energy to help you create the golden era on the surface of the Earth.

Introduction

In this teaching, Thoth explains the effortless process of growth that Earth was able to experience during the golden era. Earth's whole being, including the living beings that had a unique purpose, could experience the cosmic light constantly. All living beings experienced life in unity and as one, they received the light and went through powerful transformations. In this pure state of being, the physical body could grow as part of her cosmic, astral existence.

Wisdom of Thoth: Life on the surface of the Earth during the golden era

All human beings should bring Earth's golden era into their being. This is a powerful way to connect to the essence of Earth and purify from distortion that exists on the surface of the planet. Earth is a multidimensional being that experiences constant transformation and growth. She is a powerful creator and everything that she creates carries the same gifts, qualities, and creative powers.

In the golden era, transformation and growth were caused by the high light of the cosmos. Earth's physical body was in constant transformation. She was created to have an aura or an energy field that extended far beyond the physical body. The beings that Earth created first appeared in the core and they were light beings having an eternal life cycle, supporting Earth's growth and transformation. The beings that were created carried the light of Earth's essence and the high light of the Source and were created to receive and transmit light. Earth's intention has not changed over the years: she always creates receivers and transmitters of light.

In the golden era, Earth's intention was to remain in a state of expansion towards the high planes and have a direct and open connection with the Source. Earth was created to be the seed of a new high plane that could support the expansion of the astral plane.

Introduction

Earth is a powerful healer and when human beings connect to her light and physical body, they receive her healing energy in their whole being. This is a clear sign that Earth and humanity exist in unity; all growth, beauty, and greatness that exists in the core of the Earth can spread to every energy point throughout her whole creation. When Earth goes through a purification process, all beings who breathe on the planet will purify with Earth as one being.

Wisdom of Thoth: Earth's purification process

When you connect to Earth, you can experience a feast of sensations, looking at beautiful lands, smell the flowers and trees, hear the natural sounds, taste the healing plants and fruit and touch countless textures in the form of a living being. You are very relaxed and content being in nature; you experience balance within your being, your mind is less active and you exist in unity with Earth and her creation.

Earth has a great healing effect on you and this effect can be magnified if you are able to connect to her energies. You can connect to Earth's energies wherever you are. They blend with your aura, they support and nourish your whole being. This is happening because you are part of Earth's energy field and Earth is naturally supporting you to grow and receive the light of the cosmos.

Everything that Earth creates is energy points in this field. Its core is in the inner Earth and spreads out to the surface and to the aura of the planet. All living beings are receivers and transmitters of light. This brings growth to the Earth's field and supports her abilities to create. Earth is going into a purification process and when this is completed the high energies of the core of the Earth will expand to her whole being and replace the low frequencies and the distortion.

You are part of this purification process. Humanity has to connect to the light of the cosmos and this will open a channel for the high energies of the Earth to spread and heal all beings. You should focus on healing yourself, purify from imbalances, and become pure light in you. This will guide you to be a perfect transmitter and receiver of the cosmic light.

Introduction

This teaching explains the importance of people to consciously experience growth in unity with Earth and all creation. Knowing your path and fulfilling your growth depends on escaping the restrictions and illusions of the ego and mind and entering into space where all cosmic creation is united. Live your life knowing that all life, planes, guides, gods, the cosmic light, and the source are part of your being.

Wisdom of Thoth: All life exists in divine unity

Human beings know gods through mythology and religion. For many humans, a god has a physical as well as a light form and he or she is concerned about the lives of human beings. When human beings are not able to experience unity, they cannot see that they are part of a living god and this is Earth but they are also part of a high creator and this is the Source.

The greatest illusion and suffering that humans experience is their illusionary belief that they exist separately from Earth and if Gods exist, they are only concerned about the human civilization which is superior and therefore in separation from all creation. This belief makes humans receive and transmit illusion, focus on the mind/ego, and experience a life disconnected from their purpose and path.

When you connect to Earth and see how effortlessly she can create and nourish all living beings, you will know that she is a god creator following cosmic laws. Earth is connected to the cosmos, she is experiencing cosmic growth and she wants all her creation to exist in unity and create a bridge for the cosmic light to enter her energy field.

The purpose of humanity is to become creators and experience their divine plan, the godly plan. When you are able to connect to Earth, connect to the cosmos, follow cosmic laws, and create effortlessly then you experience the high light of the cosmos transforming your being.

Some of you may want to know about the gods of the Pleroma. You may also want to ask: can humans be gods? The gods of the pleroma exist in high light and they are able to connect to the Source and create according to the Source's intention.

A simple way to explain the Source and its connection to the gods and the rest of the creation is the following: Imagine a human being that is fully naked, this human being would want to cover himself in order to feel safe, warm, and protected. He may also want to develop some tools to help him create. Then he is going to create his home, his garden, his neighborhood, town, or country. The intention of this being is the light of the Source; the clothes and tools are the gods of the pleroma; his home and garden are the high planes where gods exist and everything else is the rest of the creation. The light of the Source is guiding the gods to create. This light is absolute unity and absolute freedom.

Wisdom of Thoth: Enlightenment a gift to humanity

Enlightenment was a gift given to beings in the lower planes to help them connect to the high energies that exist in the cosmos and Earth. Human beings can have multiple enlightenment experiences that help their being open up to the unity, vastness, and power of the cosmos to grow and expand constantly.

Human beings are locked in a reality of fear and limitation. This supports distortion, schisms, separation, and trauma. Enlightened beings are not superior. They are the ones who are connecting to their being, experiencing their truth, and co-creating their path. People should open themselves to the opportunities that were created by their divine plan and experience them in their everyday life. Heal the schisms, nourish your whole being with peace and the knowing of your divine plan. Then enlightenment is a joyful and effortless process that opens you up to receive and become the cosmos.

Introduction

There was a time that gods were able to communicate with the people of Earth and sacred wisdom was passed down to them. It was necessary that the Earth should return to her first phase of growth, her golden era. Gods shared sacred knowledge and high light with the priests and wise men of different communities to help people escape survival and return to effortless growth. The priests created temples that had high energies for people to visit and receive healing, acquire knowledge, restore balance and connect to the gods' energies. The ceremonies and rituals often took place in rural areas in order to heal Earth from her trauma. The teachings of the gods were communicated to people energetically; musical harmonies and dance were also used, imitating the harmonies of the cosmos.

Wisdom of Thoth: The enormous potential of self

Human beings tried to safeguard sacred knowledge in order to protect it from distortion, destruction and death. Many leaders and practitioners of the arts of manipulation were attracted to this knowledge that they thought would help them empower themselves and connect them to high beings. Many expeditions and wars took place on Earth for people of power to acquire sacred knowledge.

The place of The City of Shambhala (Tibet) was a mystery school connected to other mystery schools that existed in the areas of Europe and Asia. Many of those mystery schools were invaded and destroyed and their members had to take sanctuary in remote areas that were less accessible. The people who lived there were students and teachers of cosmic truth. They were all connected to the high energies of Earth and this made it possible for them to connect to the cosmos.

All people who lived there understood cosmic truths and they all participated in rituals. Wisdom was not a privilege but a gift to all beings who are able to connect to the light of the cosmos and understand their purpose. The purity and connection that those people were able to experience then are now diminished and altered because they accepted visitors who were against growth.

You are asking me if there is an entrance in this area that leads to the hollow Earth. Human beings cannot enter the hollow Earth. You can use telepathy to connect to beings that exist there; you can have visions of it. The first living beings that were created by Earth and experienced the Golden age, they now live in the hollow Earth to protect themselves from destruction.

Many people are interested in reading about mystery schools and the knowledge and growth they shared with their members. I will advise you not to follow the illusion by fantasizing about what you cannot experience yourself. Do not divide people into masters and students; you can not be a master if you are not a student. Growth is constant and mastery is an illusion. Everything that exists on Earth and the cosmos is in you and you have to focus on the enormous potential of self. Allow the transformation to take place, allow your light to transform others.

CHAPTER II

THE SACRED BOOK OF EARTH

Introduction

The following teaching will take you on a journey to the astral plane. All beings that exist in the cosmos have a creation-code and this is the seed of our Source that created your being. The creation code exists as part of the Source and is able to generate different forms of life that can expand and transform. These forms of life are created in the astral plane with the light of our Source and the creative powers of the Gods, working together as one to create life.

The astral plane is divided into different sub-planes and this supports the different types of growth and purpose of the beings that occupy it. At the same time, all subplanes are connected by cosmic laws and by the light of creation. The astral body is not physical but it is an energy form that is in constant transformation and experiences everlasting growth.

The following teaching will offer knowledge about the time that Earth was an astral being and had no experience as a physical body. There was a time that Earth did not have to participate in a planetary movement around the sun or to support the growth of her physical body; she was an astral being in the astral plane and her duty was to support its expansion so it can become a powerful laboratory for cosmic creation. The astral plane's expansion created a number of sub-planes that initially supported the cosmic creation in the astral plane but later on, grew to have their own unique growth and experience some independence from the astral plane.

Wisdom of Thoth: Earth, a Light Being

Earth's physical body went through countless transformations and cycles of growth. Before the creation of the physical body, Earth was a light being and supported the expansion of the astral plane, this means that she was a receiver and transmitter of light and supported life, growth, higher light spreading to the astral plane that will support expansion and the creation of new life. There was not a divine plan that Earth will have a physical body. She was supporting the power of the cosmic light to create layers of cosmic existence so the astral plane can become a powerful laboratory of life.

The subplanes that surrounded the astral plane supported its growth and its ability to create various energy fields and eventually become a complex organism. Some of the subplanes became planes that had different vibrations and started to exist as separate beings with their own laws and creation. The new planes were seen as an interesting experiment allowing new life to be created and new energy fields to be built.

Some of these planes became the home of a unique form of growth and transformation, the physical body. All life that was created there experienced some form of separation from the cosmic creation, the astral plane, the cosmic light, and the Source. It was the Source's intention that the cosmic light traveled to all planes, bringing life to all energy fields and light beings. The cosmic light is always teaching you that there is unity and through unity there is growth.

Introduction

The following teaching explains the existence of the new subplanes and how their unique growth initiated a series of transformations that led to the creation of physicality. The creation of the physical existence was seen as a unique process that will allow beings to experience life not only as light and energy but also as a physical body of different densities.

The creation of this new form of life will be supported by a tidal wave of high transformation processes created by the light of the source, moving to the core of the astral plane and directed to the subplanes that now have become the new laboratory that will create the physical existence. This unique opportunity of growth was created to strengthen, balance, and expand the astral body and the cosmic creation as a whole.

Wisdom of Thoth: New planes and the creation of physical existence

The growth and expansion of the astral plane affect the growth of all beings. It affects their rebirth and regeneration. I know that human beings want to define everything with the linear time that is used on Earth right now but this is an illusion and cannot define cosmic creation. Even your understanding of the present moment cannot define the process of cosmic growth because everything exists in unity and all life grows as one being constantly and eternally.

So the astral plane experienced growth that allowed it to expand and create many subplanes and these subplanes became separate planes having their own vibration. Earth is an astral being whose duty is to create energy bonds and connect all these planes to the core of the cosmic creation, the astral plane.

The growth opportunity that is related to the creation of the physical body was offered to the new planes to avoid a total separation from the astral plane as they enter a low vibration existence. The creation of a physical body was seen as a unique transformation: life will not be experienced only in the form of an astral being but can also carry another form.

The physicality was a unique creation and the cosmic light was eager to create many different variations of this. What was created first is a physical plane. This was a space of creation where guides, gods, planets, galaxies, and beings were able to take a physical or semi-physical form. This was seen as high growth and a great opportunity for the astral plane and cosmic light to grow.

Introduction

Energy flows through all beings throughout the cosmos. Energy is information and the purest way of communication. Everything in the universe is in constant transformation and movement. When there is transformation, the universe is alive and produces high energy able to sustain life. The cosmos seems to have a very complex structure, mainly because of its vastness and the multiple reflections of it, co-existing all at the same time.

When the astral plane experienced high activity and needed to expand, subplanes were created to carry, receive and transmit the cosmic light. During the first cycles of growth, they followed the same cosmic laws and later as they were not able to receive the high light and grow fully with the astral plane, the subplanes developed very unique characteristics. They experienced new vibrations and processes of growth that led to the creation of physical existence.

Wisdom of Thoth: Growth in the subplanes

The astral plane went through a number of transformations when the lower planes were created. They were part of the astral but very soon developed their own ways to grow and transform, absorb the light, and create. All planes are living beings; they are part of the cosmic field and one of the main centers of this field is the astral plane.

The astral plane is a powerful receiver of the light of the Source and when the astral plane transmits it, the light becomes the powerful creative force that reaches every energy point in the whole creation. When this happens the light of the Source becomes the light of the cosmos.

All planes are alive because of the light beings that support their growth. The creation of multiple subplanes affected their ability to grow, receive and transmit Light. Planes with low vibration were created and the energetic balance of the cosmos was altered.

The gods who were able to carry the light of the Source, were sent to the lower planes to stabilize energies and to maintain unity within the whole cosmic creation. This is when physical existence started to take place in the lower planes. Physicality was a new direction that will create life and maintain balance within the cosmos.

The gods were satisfied with the new forms of life in the low planes because they saw them as a new laboratory for creating life through unique processes that cannot be experienced in the astral plane. The gods were very interested in this new form of growth and supported the creation of different types of physical life, starting with the creation of star systems and planets.

This was the time that the astral being Earth was called to agree to receive a physical body and experience life in the lower planes. At this phase of growth, the lower planes were seen as the most exciting, diverse, and powerful creation. This made many light beings want to receive a physical body.

Introduction

Earth and other light beings that existed in the astral plane were given an important role: to receive and transmit light to the sub-planes and support the growth, expansion and connection with the astral plane. These light beings were chosen to create a physical body. They went through a process of intense preparation to enter the new planes and countless powerful transformations that will initiate the creation of their physical body.

Wisdom of Thoth: The new planes and the creation of the physical beings

Earth was not the only living being that experienced a physical transformation; there were many other light beings that created their own physical body and formed these new planes that were an extension of the astral plane.

For a while, Earth had to focus on the growth of her physical body but she was also guided to start a communication with other living beings and create an energy field that was supporting all new life.

When a body is in a process of evolution, it is going to receive and generate more light. There is a great movement of energies, connecting to the cosmic light and also connecting to other beings and energetic forms. The movement supports growth and creation.

There was a constant movement that supported communication between the physical beings, connection with the astral plane and the high light of the Source, and the ability to accelerate growth in the new planes. The new planes needed balance and this was part of their growth.

Introduction

In this teaching, Thoth explains that the new planes experienced a unique form of creation that was never experienced in the astral plane. This was due to the diversity and individuality of the countless physical bodies, the multiple transformations and the ways they received and transmitted the light. New laws allowed astral beings to create physical life in their own unique way.

Wisdom of Thoth: The processes of growth in the astral plane

The growth that was experienced in the new planes slowly took a different path from the processes of growth and creation in the astral plane. In the astral plane, everything exists in unity and individual growth is always supporting collective growth. The creation of the new planes followed similar patterns but the diversity and uniqueness of the physical body led to a new form of individuality and uniqueness.

This new form of growth was supported by new laws that allowed astral beings to create physical life in their own unique way. New groupings and divisions started to appear and multiple physical forms with their own unique characteristics were created on different planets and astral systems.

Earth's creation followed the astral laws initially and later there was an explosion of life that created many life forms. The whole physical body of Earth was created to nourish all these life forms. A point of high growth was experienced by Earth when she was able to create beings that were able to receive and transmit light. These beings carried the light of Earth's astral body and the physical body went through many transformations over the different cycles of growth. At this time there was not a clear distinction between animals, plants, water/land formations, or elements.

These high energy beings will have certain privileges as well as duties: becoming creators themselves and sharing their light to support Earth's creation and growth. Earth will give responsibilities and engage all life in processes of growth and transformation in order to empower and link the physical creation with the astral plane.

Introduction

Earth's physical body was created by the light of the Source received by the gods creators. The light, that can be described as a powerful and effortless flow, exists in the cosmic energy field and the light of Earth's astral body supports the godly creation. The physical body went through many energy exchanges to receive the high light of creation that caused the birth of many different life forms.

The creation of life forms on Earth's physical body altered her creative intention and affected the balanced coexistence between all the beings that existed on the planet. Earth experienced an explosion of life in her whole physical body: a mixture of microorganisms, plants, animals, elements, waters, mountain formations, and entrances that will give access to all different layers to the whole Earth's body.

Wisdom of Thoth: Earth's transformation

In the golden era, all beings were fully connected to Earth and were able to participate in all processes of growth and transformation because they saw themselves as an extension of Earth's physical and astral body. Earth's creative force will allow them to be in constant regeneration and rebirth, receiving the high light of the cosmos into their being and supporting the vast energy field that united all life.

This type of creation was experienced in many planets and allowed them to slowly build their own natural laws, focus on unique processes of growth in order to support the creation, and experience some independence from the growth in the astral plane, following new planetary laws. Each planet had its own laws and they supported creation processes, growth of individual life forms, and ways to balance individual, collective purpose and divine plan.

Earth's physical body was created by the divine creative flow, that is powerful and effortless, guided by the cosmic light and the light of her astral body. The birth of many different life forms altered her creative intention and affected the balanced coexistence between all the beings that existed on Earth. There was a moment on Earth's growth during the golden era that her whole physical body was touched by life, forming a mixture of microorganisms, plants, animals, elements, waters, mountain formations, and entrances to give access to all different layers to communicate and living beings to enter whole Earth's body. Earth's constant transformation supported her creative abilities but soon she was about to go on a diversion.

Introduction

Earth's physical body was fully created during the golden era. At that time, Earth was able to nourish and protect the lives of countless life forms. The divine light that came to Earth during the golden era, supported the life and the constant transformation of these beings. The light of the source and the godly intervention supported Earth to create receivers and transmitters of light. The focus of the living beings was to experience unity with the whole Earth's harmonious coexistence and have an individual path and purpose supporting their own being and all life on Earth.

Wisdom of Thoth: Earth, the creator of the golden era

Earth and other planets were allowed to create their own natural laws to support the physical body and the life forms that were created. The natural laws gave more opportunities for growth and offered a new gift: the gift of individual purpose.

When this natural law was accepted by Earth and her creation, they all entered a new phase of growth. During the Golden

Era, Earth had fully created her physical body. She was able to nourish and protect the lives of many life forms and this made her a proud and fulfilled creator. The divine light that came to Earth during the golden era, supported the life of the beings that were created on the planet. The focus of the living beings was to experience unity with the whole Earth's harmonious coexistence and have an individual path and purpose supporting their own being and all life on Earth.

At the beginning of the Golden Era, life forms went through constant transformation and their physical body did not fully resemble either animals or plants. What was created first was the light of a being attached to an individual energy field and a physical body that was in constant transformation. In this physical body, there was no mind. Communication, coexistence, and growth were happening through the energy field of each being.

Introduction

In this teaching, Thoth explains the creation of the Earth's physical body. The gods created her physical body by connecting to the Source, Earth's creation code and the light of her astral body. An astral seed will give birth to the physical body through constant transformation.

The new being will be supported by new energy fields that will support the growth in the physical body. Links between the physical and the astral body were also created. The first physical bodies that were created were the planes with their planets and astral systems. At first Earth's position was in a plane close to the astral having a similar vibration with their astral body and able to create life herself being a goddess creator.

Wisdom of Thoth: The creation of Earth's physical body

When Earth was called to enter the new planes and receive guidance to support the creation of her physical body, she was also given the opportunity to transform into a demi-god, connecting to the light of our Source and becoming a creator. Many astral beings experienced this transformation, having a physical body and they are also creators to help the physical life grow.

You may want to know how Earth, having an astral form, was able to transform into a physical being and still maintain her astral existence. It was decided that astral beings can have a physical body and this is seen as another layer of life. So beings can experience life in different planes having different layers of existence that they are all connected and support the collective growth of the cosmos.

When light beings are able to have a life experience as a physical body not only they support their growth but they support the lower planes to expand, receive the light and bring transformation to the whole cosmic creation. The gods were connected to the Source and to the creation code to all these beings who wanted to transform and have an experience as a physical being. This was a very unique and powerful moment in the life of the cosmos. The creation of the gods expanded in the lower planes focusing on a new project, the physical body.

The birth of a physical body is initiated by receiving light from the astral body and the creation code and placed into the lower planes absorbing the energies. There is an astral substance that can help the creation of a physical body through transformation.

New energy fields had to be created in order to produce energies that will support the physical body. Links between the physical and the astral body were also created and unique purposes linked to the life of the physical body. The first physical bodies that were created were the planes with their planets and astral systems. At first Earth's position was in a plane close to the astral having a similar vibration with their astral body and able to create life herself being a goddess creator.

Introduction

In the first phase of growth, Earth experienced a semi-physical body which later will become the core of her physical body. Through her physicality, she was able to connect and communicate with other light beings who were going through the same transformation. The cosmic light and the new physical beings created this new cosmic existence with the intention to bring more life and growth to these planes.

Wisdom of Thoth: New life in the new planes

For Earth to create her physical body she had to go through many powerful transformations and many phases of growth as she was transforming in unity with all life in the new planes. It was a new life that was emerging, and all beings that were involved were transforming all at the same time supporting the new creation that was planted in the cosmos.

During the first phase of growth, Earth was transformed into a semi-physical body which consisted of her core connecting to other light beings that were also becoming the new physical creation of the cosmos. There was an intense movement at the core of the Earth and an external energetic movement that helped her fulfill her divine plan, becoming a physical being and a creator and at the same time supporting and communicating with other beings on the same path.

The gods were not planning to create galaxies and planets as you know them. The cosmic light and the new physical beings created this new cosmic existence with the intention to bring more life and growth to these planes. At that time the new planes that eventually slowed down the growth of the physical body, were not seen as lower planes. They were the new expansion of the astral plane that has the ability to create new life through new processes of growth. For some time, Earth did not expand further than her core and this is how she experienced her physical existence.

Introduction

During her transformations, Earth was always surrounded and supported by the light of the Source, the intention of the gods, and other creative forces that are active in the astral plane and can spread to the new planes. The core was the first form of physicality that Earth has ever experienced and she always accepted it as her true physical body and all other parts as an expansion of the core. The gods created a new divine plan for Earth and gave her new abilities to create so her physical form could expand. She understood her purpose as a creator and saw this as a gift given only to high creator gods.

Wisdom of Thoth: Earth's core

In the first phase of her growth, Earth was able to experience a semi-physical core surrounded by the light of the Source, the light of the gods, and other creative forces that supported her during her transformation. These high energies gave Earth support and protection to help her continue with her transformation process.

For Earth, her physical body is her core and all other layers are the expansion of the core. This reflects the astral plane and the creation of the other subplanes: a natural expansion whose purpose was to bring more growth and unity. When the core of the Earth was created, the gods created a new divine plan for Earth and gave her new abilities to create so her physical form and growth could expand. She understood her purpose as a creator and saw this as a gift given only to high creator gods.

Looking at the core of the Earth, you will see that there were different elements created there to help Earth maintain life in the physical form. These elements cannot be found at the surface of the planet. Human beings have access to them when they connect to the core energetically and allow the high energies of the planet to enter their being.

Earth went through countless transformations from the time that her physical body was created and her elements went through various transformations too and this strengthened her creative ability. When Earth was able to experience life through her physical core, she became aware that physical creation was spreading in many planes and that she was called to become a creator herself.

Introduction

Earth experienced the birth of her physical body as an extension of her astral being and she saw it growing, transforming, receiving the light of the cosmos, and eventually having a life of its own. The astral being Earth was observing the creation of the physical body and she directed the high light of the cosmos into her physicality to support its growth and expansion. All light beings in the new planes that went through a transformation to experience a new form of existence, a physical body, were able to exist in both states, the physical and the astral.

Wisdom of Thoth: Connecting the astral existence to the physical body

The astral being Earth gave birth to the core of the planet that became her physical body. At that time all light beings that went through a transformation to experience a new form of existence, a physical body, were able to exist in both states, the physical and the astral.

Earth experienced the birth of her physical body as an extension of her astral being and she saw it growing, receiving the light of the cosmos, and eventually having a life of its own. The astral being Earth was observing her physical body and she directed the high light of the cosmos into her physicality to grow and expand.

All astral beings that were able to experience their physicality, brought light to the new planes and helped them support new life forms. All the gods of the pleroma and other light beings were part of this new creation, they supported the light to enter the new physical forms, strengthen and multiply opportunities of growth in these beings as well as the planes.

You may ask what is a plane? A plane is a unique energy field that has its own vibration, the process of growth, the ability to receive light, and unique life forms. The new planes were not fully grown yet so the new life that was created needed the support of all god creators. Earth's core was a high vibrational planet ready to grow and experience life that was unique.

Introduction

This teaching offers valuable information about the creation of the core of Earth. It was created by an astral substance that exists in the new planes and has a lower vibration than the light that exists in the astral plane. Through a number of transformations and with the support of the cosmic light, this substance could take a semi-physical form and will form the core of the physical body. The core would be the most precious, the most protected part that will maintain the highest energies and all life will be generated and spread from there.

Wisdom of Thoth: The creation of the core of the Earth

You may want to know more about Earth's core at the beginning of its creation. It was created by an astral substance that exists in the new planes. This substance has a lower vibration than the light that exists in the astral plane, therefore can transform into a semi-physical substance with the support of the cosmic light, the intention of our source, and the creative abilities of the gods.

The first element that was created had a form of air which was a carrier of light and supported the creation of a grid, starting from the core of the Earth and expanding to the outer parts. After many transformations, part of this air substance took a liquid form and this was when Earth became a creator. In this liquid core, Earth started to create using the light of the cosmos, her own creative abilities, the support of the gods, and the guidance of her divine plan.

Earth was able to see her physical body and ways to maintain life. She understood that the core would be the most precious, the most protected part that will maintain the highest energies and all life will be generated and spread from there.

One of the important creations of Earth was the grid that can also be seen as an extended energy field that is covering all parts of her physical body as well as the energies that surround this physical body. Earth's aura was the high light of the gods that carried the Source's intention and all the creative energies of the cosmos. This grid was created to support and protect the new physical being and to maintain a connection between the astral body and the physical body of Earth. So both bodies existed in the same plane and had the same growth.

Introduction

The core of Earth's physical body became a powerful laboratory where Earth will go on multiple transformations, create elements, living beings, grow her physical body and stay connected to the astral body that is a receiver of the high light of the cosmos.

Air and water were the first elements created in the core and through them, Earth created living beings that became the seed for the growth and expansion of her physical body. Another important development was the creation of channels and entrance points on Earth's body for the light of the cosmos to move in and spread to her whole being.

Wisdom of Thoth: The first elements created in the core of the Earth

During the creation of her physical body, Earth focused on the creative activity of the core and the birth of different elements. First, the air element was created, followed by the water element. The air element was more of an energy field than a physical form and was able to carry light.

Earth's creative powers grew when the water element appeared in her core and many life forms were created. If human beings were able to experience life in a pure state, they would remember Earth's transformations and they would be able to create the way she creates.

The air and water elements that started to form in Earth's physical body, created living beings that became the seed for the growth and expansion of Earth's physical body. She created openings for the light of the cosmos to enter her physical body and channels within the body to help the light spread and be received by her whole being.

She created a grid that will support this process. The grid will start from her astral being entering the core of her physical body to expand to outer planes where the light of the gods had created another grid of high light connecting to the Source. The core of Earth's physical body is a place full of light because it is directly connected to Earth's astral body.

Introduction

Earth's duties as a new creator were the following: to transform her physical body into a receiver and transmitter of light, to create a multi-layered physical body that has the ability to expand and grow and to support the creation of the new plane and its unique growth. All physical beings in the new plane should be supported and protected by all life and this will create stability and opportunities of growth for the whole cosmic creation.

Wisdom of Thoth: The creation of planets

When Earth and other light beings created their physical body, they also created a new plane that allowed light beings to experience this new process of growth having a physical body.

Some of you may ask how Earth was formed into a planet and not another physical being? It is because Earth and a number of other light beings were the first to experience physicality therefore became a physical planet that will sustain and offer the physical experience to other light beings.

For a long time reincarnation was not a process of growth for light beings. Earth's astral body was fully connected to her physical body and in the core, she received the cosmic light and the creative intention of the gods that allowed her to be a creator.

The core was not anymore Earth's physical body but it was the seed that could transform into the physical body into Earth that you know in your time. The core of the Earth was always a powerful receiver and transmitter of light. It was energized by the light of the Source to receive its intention in the same way as gods do.

Earth had more special duties: to transform her physical body into a receiver and transmitter of light, to create a multi-layered physical body, and to support the creation of a new plane that has unique growth.

The energies of the core created a field that followed the cosmic laws and was a reflection of the cosmic field. This supported Earth to grow her physical body and create its elements.

Introduction

All human beings that experience life on the surface of the Earth in the present moment, should connect to Earth's energies and experience the power of the planet's core. This unique connection will expand their understanding of Earth's ability to grow, transform, and create life. It is their opportunity to experience the golden era that still exists in the core and make it their truth.

Wisdom of Thoth: Effortless Growth

Earth saw her core as a laboratory where all light enters to create, empower and transform life. What Earth was able to create first in the core of her being were elements that she will later use for to generate life in her physical being. Her core went through countless phases of rebirth to be able to take a physical form that can generate many layers and a plethora of living beings.

The human beings who live on the surface of the Earth in the present moment, have a very limited understanding of Earth's being and all her stages of growth, the birth processes and metamorphosis that created the Earth-physical being that they are used to. They are not able to see and experience the core of the planet, its creative energies and the living beings who exist there and continue to grow. If they were able to experience this, they would have full awareness of Earth's creation and transformation.

In this present moment in the core of the Earth, the golden era is a current experience. The high energies of the cosmos, the high light of the Source, and the astral existence of Earth are connected to the core and they are responsible for its constant transformation and the creation of elements, nutrients, high energies, and the maintenance of the energy field that allows Earth to be a receiver and transmitter of light.

At the beginning of Earth's evolution, growth was happening effortlessly and multiple transformations shaped Earth's body. Her physical body was growing because it was in constant and direct connection with the high creative forces of the cosmos.

Because of this connection, her ability as a creator expanded and the core of her being became a womb for living beings to be created and life to enter Earth's elements.

Introduction

When Earth became a creator in the new planes, she became aware of her new divine plan, purpose and path. She knew that all astral beings that were able to experience a physical existence, were a magnet for the cosmic light to support their growth. She also knew that the growth of her physical body was going to be linked to the growth in the new planes that are unique and different from the astral plane. All astral beings that created their physical bodies will be responsible for the creation of a new plane.

Wisdom of Thoth: The creators in the astral plane

Earth gave birth to her physical body, allowing the creative energies of the cosmos to enter her being and start a series of transformations. In the core of her physical body, elements were created so Earth could become a creator herself.

At first, Earth experienced her physical body as an extension of her astral being that followed the same cosmic laws. When the elements were created in the core, Earth was allowed to create in her physical body layers of life and new energy fields. The new life on Earth's physical body supported by new natural laws.

Earth was surrounded by other astral beings that were going through similar transformations in order to create and balance their physical bodies. Therefore a new grid was created and a new set of cosmic laws shaped life in the new plane that was going through major transformations, affecting all life forms. Earth had also created a new grid to allow light to travel to her new body and move throughout the new plane.

When Earth was called to create life within her physical body, she knew that her physicality is going to be linked to a purpose and a path and the new plane is going to have a life that is unique and different from the astral plane. All astral beings that created the physical bodies with the support of the cosmic creators were going to become creators themselves and not only will be responsible for the creation of a new body but they would also be responsible for the creation of a new plane.

Introduction

The human mind will find it hard to comprehend the cycles of growth and transformation that can be experienced by astral beings. The mind may find it challenging to consciously support transformation in the whole being. They have to be reminded that they are created to be Earth's receivers and transmitters of light. When human beings are suffering from imbalances, they are still able to connect to the cosmic light but imbalances act as a blockage for balance and growth.

Human beings have to purify themselves. This means that they have to face the imbalance and observe the way it was created and all its different forms. Having a pure intention to connect to your true self, the cosmic light will guide you and help you to purify your whole being. This experience will bring transformation to your being because you are openingup to the light and you are co-creating a new balanced existence for you. If you do not have a pure intention and you are not focusing on truth then the imbalance will remain and it is possible that it will expand and grow.

What we can learn from this is that transformation is an effortless path without disruptions, insecurities, fears, limitations and illusionary beliefs. When we accept transformation as an effortless path, we will achieve the greatness of our divine plan.

Wisdom of Thoth: Transformation in the new planes

Some of you may ask how was Earth able to create her physical body? What was the force that supported her to become a creator?
All light beings who entered this new plane and accepted the opportunity to create physical reality went through a long

preparation that was guided by the gods and the cosmic light that is the Source's intention for creation. They experienced transformations that allowed them to enter the new planes and accept the new opportunity of growth: the creation of the physical body.

All beings that created a physical body with Earth in this new plane, all followed the same cosmic laws and were supported as well as supporting others during their transformation.

Earth started to create life in her core and she was supported by maintaining a constant connection to the high light of the Source. All creators have to connect to the high light of the Source in order to create life. The life that Earth created transformed her whole physical body and brought the golden era.

The physicality of Earth started to expand; the core expanded in order to create more opportunities for growth and creation. Earth's intention was to grow her physical body and create new layers, supporting more opportunities for growth.

Introduction

Trying to understand the way Earth was able to expand and grow her physical body beyond the core, we need to focus on the connection and light exchange between the astral and the physical existence. The astral body is an energy point in the cosmic field, a receiver of high light, and the carrier of the Source's intention. During Earth's transformations, all cosmic nourishment, guidance, and creative opportunities were transmitted from the astral body to her core for Earth to fulfill her divine plan. The astral body is a high energy portal and is connecting to another major portal in the physical body, the core.

Wisdom of Thoth: The expansion of Earth's physical body.

During the creation of Earth's physical body, the core and the elements that formed it went through countless phases of regeneration and it seemed like Earth was constantly giving birth to a new physical body. These transformations created Earth's grid, moving from the core of her being, connecting to her astral body and then creating links into the cosmic grid.

All astral beings that were in a process of creating their physical body, experienced similar opportunities of evolution and they all affected each other by transmitting energy and creating grids that supported the whole plane.

There were a series of transformations that allowed the core of the Earth to become a creator of life: the elements and the light that was stored there supported the creation of new life in Earth's physical body. This was a great moment of growth because the physical being Earth became a plane, creating and supporting new life.

The first life forms that Earth created were elements, water and minerals. Earth also created stones, crystals and microorganisms. You may want to know about Earth's ability to create and nourish her new life forms. Her physical body was attached to her astral body and was nourished by it. Her creative abilities were supported by her astral growth, the cosmic light, the intention of the source and all creator gods that were co-creating with her.

Explaining Earth's creating process, one can say that in the very beginning the core of the Earth was one element. The energy grid that was created allowed multiple transformations to take place in Earth's physical body and this had different outcomes. So the core was transformed into more elements. The constant transformation and the creation of a variety of elements created different life forms that they all had a collective purpose to transform with Earth but also the ability to have unique characteristics that will breed a variety of new life forms on Earth.

Introduction

Earth created new layers in her physical body by creating new elements that supported the creation of landscapes, water formations and other living beings. When Earth's physical body started to grow, all living beings that were part of her physical body, were able to experience a multidimensional reality. They could experience the growth of their physical existence, their energy and Earth's astral body all at the same time.

Earth being a multi-dimensional being was able to experience her astral growth, transformations on her physical body, communication with other planets that existed in the same plane as well as the ability to receive high light from gods and guides. She had the intention of a creator connecting directly to the cosmic light and the Source.

Wisdom of Thoth: Earth's multidimensional existence

Earth was creating life within her physical body and many other beings who were experiencing similar growth processes as

45

Earth, were also becoming creators, supporting their physical body to grow. The constant rebirth and metamorphosis of all these light beings created what you already know as planets, galaxies, and star systems.

People on Earth often speak about different dimensions and use different numbers and divisions to define the vibrational state "third, fourth, fifth and sixth dimension". All living beings that Earth created were part of her physical body, were able to experience a multidimensional reality. They could experience their physical body, their energy and Earth's astral body all at the same time.

Earth as a multidimensional being was able to experience her astral growth, transformations on her physical body, communication with other planets in the same plane as well as receiving guidance from the gods and guides and she was also able to have the intention of a creator connecting directly to the cosmic light and the Source.

Earth gave life to beings that could become her receivers and transmitters of light. She saw herself as a high creator that will support growth in the whole plane and she will have direct access to the Source and the cosmic light. She will be the link between the astral and the new planes and her physical body will be a new tool of creation that will support the growth of all cosmic life.

With this intention, she supported the expansion of her physical body into multiple layers that formed into physical landscapes and water formations. New elements were created to help the physicality grow and transform into many more living forms.

Introduction

All layers that were part of Earth's physical body were able to communicate and exist in unity even though each one of them experienced growth differently. All living beings that Earth created, remained connected to her astral existence; there was no separation. It was important that they all grow in unity, receive light and be able to constantly transform in order to maintain life. Earth gave the ability to every living being to become a powerful receiver and transmitter of light.

Wisdom of Thoth: Unity on Earth

Earth used the elements of the core of her physical being and the light of the Source to create living beings that became an integral part of Earth's physical body. At that time Earth did not experience the law of reincarnation; all living beings were part of the expansion of her physical body.

So all life that she was able to create was part of her being and supported the expansion of her physical body and energy grid. Earth created layers of life surrounding her core. All different layers were able to communicate with each other but each layer experienced a unique form of growth that made Earth a powerful and versatile creator.

Earth needed the support of the gods in order to balance energies and master her creative abilities. The gods supported Earth to create an aura. The aura allowed the cosmic light to enter every living being on Earth's physical body. All living beings were part of Earth's body and all of them connected to her astral existence; there was no separation. It was important that they all grow in unity, receive light and be able to constantly transform in order to maintain life. Later the Aura was also used as a protection grid. Earth gave the ability to every part of her physical body to become powerful receivers and transmitters of light.

Introduction

For her physical body to grow and expand into many layers, Earth had to create living nutrition. The living nutrients were able to go through their own transformation and create seeds with a life purpose and a life path. So now Earth was able to create living beings that had their own unique qualities but they also had a unique path and purpose. This was the beginning of a new phase of growth that was supported by the whole cosmic creation as a new and powerful form of growth that will expand and bring new light into the whole cosmic creation.

Wisdom of Thoth: Living nutrients and cosmic seeds

The elements that Earth created in the core of her physical body became her powerful tools for growth and expansion. She was guided to create living nutrients that will support her physical body and will also become the foundation for the birth and support of other living beings. These living nutrients consisted of high energy and Earth's light that brought physical growth in the core.

All living beings that were created on Earth at that time, carried the same template that reflects the light in the core of the Earth, the light of the astral body and the godly intention. They all experienced the unbreakable ropes of unity, they supported the growth of the planet and connected to Earth's astral body, they experienced their purpose, being receivers and transmitters.

The next phase of growth was for Earth to create landscapes of living nutrition. She created mountains of energy crystals, channels of energy that later were transformed into water formations. She allowed access to all layers in order for the physical body to be constantly nourished and in constant transformation and growth.

The living nutrients were able to go through their own regeneration and create seeds with a life purpose and a life path. So now Earth was able to create living beings that had their own unique qualities but they also had a unique path and purpose. This was the beginning of a new phase of growth that was supported by the whole cosmic creation. It was a remarkable and powerful period of growth that will expand and bring new light to the whole cosmic creation.

During this time Earth and all beings in the new planes went through this process of growth, creating their own bodies and were fully supported by the Source through the intervention of the gods. The gods shaped and strengthened their creative abilities and guided them through this wondrous process of birthing.

Introduction

Earth will continue to create more layers in her physical body where living beings can find their home and receive a constant flow of support and nourishment. Earth's living beings had the ability to regenerate and transform their body constantly. They were allowed to receive the cosmic light effortlessly, to receive Earth's nourishment and to be able to focus on their processes of growth. These living beings never experienced birth or death.

Wisdom of Thoth: New growth opportunities

Earth's ability to expand beyond the core of her physical body was supported by the creation of elements and living nourishment. Earth's landscape in the core went through many transformations and then she started to expand and create new layers of life. These layers were part of her physical body and in some ways, they had their own unique structure and growth opportunities.

This was an important step and enabled Earth to create a variety of living beings. The more living layers she was able to create in her physical body the more growth and creation she was able to experience.

Earth's creation followed an important law: all living beings exist in unity and are part of a field that offers constant nourishment and growth. In this field, all living beings become nourishment for all life on Earth.

Earth will continue to create more layers where living beings can find their home and receive a constant flow of support and nourishment. The form of the living beings that Earth created were in constant metamorphosis so the physical characteristics will transform all the time; this supported the creation of the many layers of Earth's physical body. Because of the constant transformation, living beings did not experience the restriction of death and they were allowed to receive the cosmic light, to connect to Earth's nourishment, and continue their countless cycles of transformation.

Introduction

Earth was constantly expanding, creating a powerful core, the laboratory of life, more layers of physicality that became the home of living beings and landscapes of living nourishment. All parts of Earth's physical body existed in unity and supported each other's growth. They were all co-creators.

Wisdom of Thoth: New life on Earth

Earth gave a special duty to the living beings that she created to be responsible and support the growth of the new layers in her physical body. In the beginning, these layers had similar energy and growth and living beings had easy access, being able to move from one to one another.

Earth was inspired to create even more layers and give to her living beings all the nourishment they needed in order to continue their limitless growth. This gave birth to a very unique relationship: living forms were created by Earth, they were part of her being but they were also co-creators. These living beings did not travel to Earth from the astral plane, they did not reincarnate. They were part of Earth's body, they carried her light and the physical form followed the constant transformation experienced by the whole planet.

There was a time that Earth stopped creating more layers in her physical body. She was instructed by the gods to focus on balancing energies, supporting life, focusing on receiving and transmitting light and supporting cosmic growth.

At that time, it became known to cosmic creators that the new planes may not be able to stay united with the astral plane and the growth that will take place there will not only follow the cosmic laws. Cosmic creators had to balance life in the new planes in new, unique ways and bring balance to all processes that bring growth to their physicality.

This brought some restrictions that supported communication between physical beings as well as groupings such as the creation of galaxies, universes and star systems. They were created in order to connect the new planes with the astral plane and maintain balance in the whole cosmic creation.

Introduction

The new planes were an extension of the astral plane but were allowed the creation of the physical body and this transformed them to a unique cosmic place. All gods focused on their new creation, carrying the intention of the source and the high light that traveled through them to support the new creation. As physical beings continued to grow and became complex organisms, new laws had to be created to support and protect the activity in the new planes.

Wisdom of Thoth: The astral plane supports the birth of the new planes

The astral plane supported the birth and growth of the new planes. The astral plane is the home of all beings and growth there is permanent and follows the cosmic laws. The new planes followed the cosmic laws but they also created new laws. This is because their growth that was experienced there was unique and created new life forms and new ways of living.

Every being-creator-planet created its own unique laws that brought their unique purpose. Every planet was created by unique elements, had a unique connection with the astral plane, and offered a unique process of growth to all living beings.

When the physical body of Earth completed the initial phases of transformation, the focus was to support the growth of life forms and how will be able to remain on Earth as living beings, what will be their purpose and what will be able to offer to the growth of Earth as a whole being.

The way the astral plane is nourishing all beings with the light of the Source, Earth nourished the beings that she created, connecting to the source, receiving the light in the core of her being, and spreading the light to all living beings. For Earth living beings are not only the animals and plants but it is everything that contains her elements.

There was no separation between beings and life forms; there was a very strong and clear connection with the Earth as an astral being transforming into a physical body. All beings on Earth experienced Earth's transformations and they knew that they are part of these transformations.

Introduction

What attracted astral beings to enter the new planes and experience a physical body was the opportunity of becoming creator and receiving the high light of the source. Earth created the core of her physical body, elements, living nutrients, layers that expanded beyond the core and countless living beings that co-created with Earth and were receivers and transmitters of light. When Earth connects to her creation, she can see her path and purpose.

Wisdom of Thoth: Earth's creation

At the beginning of the Golden Era, Earth saw herself as a creator supported by the Gods and the light of the Source. She could look through her creation and see her purpose and path. The beings that she created started to see their own purpose too. They knew that they were part of the Earth's physical body and light but they were also created to be unique in the way they grow, experience life, and communicate with Earth and the cosmos.

Many of the beings that Earth created were one of a kind; for example, each mammal was a different species. At that time beings did not procreate and their life cycles mirrored the life cycle of Earth's physical body. They were not fearful of dying; they have never experienced death or seen others going through this process. Everything around them was a source of nourishment and an opportunity for growth and transformation.

These beings were guided by Earth and the cosmic light to act in a certain way, experience their being, and have a balanced coexistence with other beings. At that time there was no free will. Beings did not have to choose, think, or plan, they accepted Earth's guidance being the creator of their physical body and all elements and physical life they can see around them. These living forms did not have needs, expectations, limitations, insecurities or fears; they saw themselves as diaphanous beings in their pure state, following their path without interruptions or confusion.

Introduction

The golden era was a high peak of creation and growth for Earth. She created a multi-layered physical body with whole landscapes of nutritional elements and living beings that can grow effortlessly being part of Earth's growth. All physical creation was supported by Earth's astral body which was a stargate to the cosmos.

Wisdom of Thoth: Earth's astral body

During the golden era, Earth was transformed into a high creator, a godly being of a great life. She continued to create life forms and resources that will nourish them in order to have eternal life on Earth.

Some of you may ask: do these life forms have an astral body? The life forms were an extension of Earth; they were part of Earth's physical body and they all connected to her astral body. There is no separation between beings that Earth created and her physical or astral body; they were all one being in constant transformation.

During the golden era, Earth completed the creation of her physical body. The beings that Earth created consisted mainly of energy and most of the nourishment that they received came from the light of the cosmos. They were able to exist in all layers of the Earth's body including the inner parts and most of them were attracted to certain elements and parts of the Earth that were rich in these elements.

The physical beings that resembled the animal kingdom did not follow mind processes: they experienced a natural process of effortless growth. All creation was connected energetically and all beings were aware of this. They were fully supported to grow on Earth.

Chapter III

All human beings can connect to the cosmic light. You can receive it when you accept that everything in the cosmos exists in unity. Human beings have also to accept that part of their purpose is to become a perfect receiver and transmitter of light and allow it to spread to humanity and Earth. The purpose of the light is to spread to all planes and living beings to maintain life.

Introduction

Humanity and Earth should unite in order to clear distortion and make the way back to the golden era. Human beings are not the rulers or the owners of Earth's resources as they want to believe but they are the extension of Earth; they are receivers and transmitters of energy that can connect Earth to the cosmos. Earth has given you your physical body and being a mother creator is able to nourish her creation and sustain life. Your physical body is part of your being whose purpose is to connect and support Earth's growth.

Wisdom of Thoth: Earth's golden era

Earth's golden era was a powerful moment of creation. Earth became the sun for all the planets of the new planes, she shared her light and supported the growth that took place in all planets.

Earth was the first planet to complete the creation of her physical body and then she focused on living beings. Earth saw them as layers of creation and she wanted every being to be unique and to carry Earth's greatness.

In the beginning, Earth's living beings did not have free will. They followed her intention and saw themselves as an extension of the living planet. As Earth created an increasing variety of life forms, she allowed them to have a unique purpose and path. When beings started to experience their unique purpose, they were guided to become creators themselves. They connected to Earth's creative force and the cosmic light and started to create.

During the Golden Era, Earth's creation experienced constant changes in the physical body and energy field and this was the right state for growth to be experienced by all beings. Earth co-created with all living beings and this gave her the position of the sun, receiving and transmitting light to all new planes.

Introduction

This teaching shares important information about Earth's creation and the ways they were able to experience life and grow. They were part of Earth's physical body and shared the same astral existence: Earth's astral body. All living beings will receive the high light of the cosmos when they enter Earth's astral body, going through the core of her physicality and then spread to every living being in order to provide nourishment and growth. Living beings were able to transmit the light and this is when they became creators themselves. That was the high peak of the golden era on Earth where all life transformed and created in unity.

Wisdom of Thoth: Creators of life

During the golden era, Earth was observing and guiding her creation to become creators themselves. She gave them their first duty to become receivers and transmitters of light. Earth and her creation were one, therefore all the light that was coming to the core of Earth's body was instantly spread to every being.

Earth's whole physical body including her living beings was fully connected to the astral body of Earth; there was no separation and all light on Earth was able to receive and transmit the cosmic light without interruptions. Earth was a goddess creator, connecting to the highlight of the cosmos and all beings on Earth were also high creators.

During this process, beings were able to create reflections of their being. This was an energetic expansion of their whole being that moved into a process of growth in order to create a separate energy field which will later form into a new physical body. This creative ability that the lifeforms on Earth were able to experience created a vast variety of species in the animal and plant kingdom and also species that have common characteristics. This high creation was the highpoint of Earth's golden era that led Earth to complete the creation of her physical body and make lifeform creators, experiencing and spreading growth which became an unstoppable force on Earth.

Introduction

Earth, during the high growth in the golden era, was a powerful creator and a transmitter of light to all other physical beings (planets) in the new planes. Other planets will connect to Earth for support when their journey to mastering creation becomes challenging. For this to happen new energy fields had to be built to support constant energy/light flow throughout the body of all planets. The divine plan for the new planes was an abundance of opportunities for growth and constant unity between all beings, having access to the astral plane as one being. This happened for a while but the separation which was unavoidable created divisions and schisms that affected the vibration and growth of the new planes.

Wisdom of Thoth: Life in the new planes

Other planets followed Earth's growth but they were more of a follower looking for support and guidance. For Earth, her process of growth was uninterrupted and effortless like a series of experiences that were all part of the divine plan but for other planets the process of growth was different and this had to do with the light of their astral body and how is it allowed to become a creative force, building this new physical body.

Earth's duty was to support the planets and the planes. It was one of the reasons why she allowed her life forms to be responsible for creation. She wanted support to be spread to all planes as well as growth to continue happening in her own being. At that time the new planes started to restructure themselves by creating connections between all life forms, strong energy fields that can carry the light and allow the cosmic light to flow effortlessly.

Later, parts of this energy field weakened, and new energy fields were created that supported the grouping of planets into galaxies and astral systems. Initially, Earth was not part of these groupings but she continued to share light and support to the new planes and have constant access to the astral plane. The groupings of these planets created a separation between the living beings of the new planes and the astral; this separation will become a schism and make the new planes, lower planes.

Introduction

The gods of the Pleroma were actively involved in the creation of the new planes spreading the light of the source. Earth was chosen by the gods to support and nourish life in the new planes. She was a powerful light carrier and transmitter and her purpose was not only to experience growth in her being but to support growth in other beings. Earth was able to fulfill her purpose but not all planets were able to do the same. This led to the creation of more subplanes that had different vibrations and allowed a different form of growth. These new subplanes were created to support living beings, planets that experienced slow growth but eventually created separation and scisms.

Wisdom of Thoth: The creation

During the Golden era, Earth did not experience any schisms. Her being was the highest energy point of all creation in the new planes. Physicality was not a limitation and the high light of the Source could travel to all life on Earth without restrictions or interruptions. Earth created many grids that will help her receive and transmit light to every part of her being and she also empowered all her creation to become receivers and transmitters of light so growth is never interrupted or blocked.

All beings in the cosmic creation should connect to the Source through the cosmic light. The gods that existed in the pleroma were the ones that created and supported life so their purpose was to become part of the Source's creative force and take any steps necessary for the creation to be in constant growth.

The gods were actively involved in the creation of the new planes and gave Earth an important place, guiding and supporting not only her own growth but the growth of all living beings in all planes. Not all planets were able to grow and fulfill their purpose, therefore, more subplanes were created that had a different vibration and allowed a different form of growth. These new subplanes were created to support living beings, planets that experienced slow growth but eventually this will create separation and scisms. This is how the low vibrational planes were created.

Introduction

Earth was given the role of a stargate, a portal, for the cosmic light to enter the new planes and support the growth of the planets. Earth became a being of high light and all physical bodies wanted to receive the light in order to complete their cycles of growth. Planets received guidance, support, healing and growth opportunities when they connected to Earth and the light that she transmitted.

Wisdom of Thoth: Earth becoming a stargate

Earth observed the creation of the subplanes, the slow growth of the planets and the divisions that started to emerge and she became a stargate in the new planes, fulfilling her purpose as a receiver and transmitter of light. The high light of the cosmos will enter her being, will be transmitted to the new planes and support all life.

Earth allowed the light to travel through her energy field and support all life in the new planes. Earth was experiencing a high point of growth and was called to share the growth of the golden era with other living beings in order to stop divisions and schisms from happening in the new planes.

Earth became a being of high light and all physical bodies moved around it to receive it. Planets received guidance, support, healing and growth opportunities when they connected to Earth and the light that she transmitted. Earth could share the light of the gods, the light of the source and be a point of connection among all life in the new planes.

Some of you may ask: what went wrong and other planets could not experience a golden era? There are many different factors: the physical body may experience separation from the astral body and this can lead to many imbalances including the inability to receive fully and effortlessly the light of the source. In some cases, the physical body existed almost separate and without guidance from the astral body.

Imbalances can be created when the astral body is not ready to create a physical body or it needs to go into a longer preparation for this task. Furthermore, they may be certain phases of the physical body's growth that were not completed. The growth in the new planes was an experiment and now it is absolutely necessary for the Gods to intervene, support and guide with their high light.

Introduction

Earth was a powerful creator and was given a very important duty: this was to become a meeting point for all life on Earth to connect to the high light of the gods. All living beings that were part of Earth's creation, supported her in fulfilling her duty, becoming the receivers and transmitters of light. Earth was experiencing a new phase of growth, allowing her creation to explore free will and become creators.

Wisdom of Thoth: A new cycle of growth for Earth

Earth's intervention was to support the gods to bring balance and opportunities of growth and correction whenever is needed in the new planes. Powerful energy fields were created in an area of growth that consisted of many sub-planes of different vibrations and a variety of growth opportunities. The creation of a more effective energy field brought unity to the new planes.

Earth was experiencing a new phase of growth, allowing her creation to explore free will in order to become creators. In the beginning, the elements were the only living beings on the planet that could be used to create life. The light of Earth created lots of different forms that consisted of the elements of the physical planet. These life forms transformed with the planet and finally were able to fully experience life with their physical body and become creators themselves. This was the beginning of a new phase where Earth's beings were given the opportunity to create and support the growth of the planet.

All living beings on Earth were receivers and transmitters of light and supported Earth to become a meeting point for all life in the new planes, meeting the gods of the pleroma and receiving support by the cosmic light and the source.

Introduction

In the golden era, the living beings on Earth were not divided into the groups and families known to us in the present time. All living beings experienced unity with Earth and they were aware that the essence of their physical body exists in the core

of the Earth. The physical body of the beings that existed on Earth cannot be defined because some of them can share characteristics of a plant as well as an animal but they were also other forms that we have no reference of for example beings that parts of their being are crystals, water or light formations

Wisdom of Thoth: The essence of a being

Earth's creation during the golden era was not divided into different kingdoms such as the animal or the plant kingdom. There was a powerful unity that supported all creation and this brought constant growth and transformation. The light of a being which is also its essence was prominent and existed in the core of the Earth that was surrounded by layers of physicality and energy. The physical body of the beings that existed on Earth was a mixture of plant-animal but they were also living forms that cannot be compared to any form that is known to you.

Earth created unique life forms this means that each life form was one of the kind and later when Earth beings became creators they were able to allow the creation and growth of new beings that carried their uniqueness.

You may ask how did they achieve this? This was a new phase of growth that Earth had to experience: to allow her creation to grow and multiply. Earth as a whole had a new intention: to focus on collective growth, regenerating her elements, connecting to the light of the Source, focusing on her divine plan and the instructions of the gods as well as supporting the new planes to grow. Earth's high light had to be shared with all creation in the new planes because the schisms and the appearance of more subplanes could affect the growth of all beings in these planes. So Earth's creation was encouraged to co-create with her and this brought the planet to the high peak moment during the Golden era.

Introduction

The planets in all subplanes went through a period of balance and unity. There was a time of regeneration and rebirth in the new planes that was supported by the light of the cosmos. Earth's physical body, on the other hand, experienced a rapid expansion. Families of life forms were created and the plant kingdom expanded fast and in the most versatile way. The plant kingdom was called to become the "mother" of Earth's creation, nourishing, healing, supporting the growth of all beings on the planet. The plant kingdom accepted this important role and was rewarded with everlasting growth that is effortless and a gift to all.

Wisdom of Thoth: High Growth

During the peak of Earth's golden era, gods and beings of high light existed on Earth. She was chosen to be a powerful light, co-creator, and high guide of all activity in the new planes. When beings accept a cosmic duty, they are rewarded and one of these rewards is to be supported by the great light of the source coming through the gods and the high beings of cosmic growth.

While Earth supported all creation in the new planes to receive light, heal schisms and renew energy fields and grids, she experienced a cycle of high growth that transformed her whole being and all living beings that are part of her.

Earth was experiencing a high peak of growth and at the same time, the planets in all subplanes went through a period of balance and unity. There was a time of regeneration and rebirth in the new planes that was supported by the light of the cosmos.

The number and variety of life forms on Earth increased rapidly. Families of life forms were created, the plant kingdom expanded much faster and in the most versatile way. The plant kingdom became the "mother" of Earth's creation, nourishing, healing, supporting the growth of all beings on the planet. The plants accepted this important role and were rewarded with everlasting growth that is effortless and a gift to all.

CHAPTER IV

When you are distorted you have no clarity, you have no connection to your true-self. In this confused state you cannot see your purpose; you cannot allow yourself to walk your path and live an effortless life according to your divine plan. When many people are affected by distortion they all exist in this space of confusion and they convince each other that this is a natural way to experience life on Earth. When you finally see the truth, you will see distortion as a dark cloud that blocks your understanding. Opening up to the cosmic light can help you blow this cloud away and heal the trauma, schisms and unpurified parts of your being.

Introduction

Earth's growth in the golden era moved from one high peak to the next and the planet was able to sustain and expand its creation. For the planets in the subplanes, high growth was not constant. They were able to create living beings that had free will but this led to schisms. A sign of the schism was the confusion and the uncertainty that beings on other planets started to experience.

Wisdom of Thoth: Schisms in the new planes

The Golden Era on Earth expanded to many cycles of growth and Earth experienced immense power to create her own physical body and support life in the new planes. During the Golden Era, Earth transformed into a complex organism and her creation experienced a unique purpose and path having their own creative abilities. Their new purpose was based on free will.

There were other planets in the new planes that were also able to create life forms whose process of growth led them to become creators and have free will. This was the beginning of the many schisms between the planet-body and its creation and the low vibrational growth that was about to become a reality for all life in the new planes.

A sign of the schism was the confusion and the uncertainty that beings started to experience. The connection between the physical and the astral body became weaker and the cosmic support that was needed to flow through the planet to support constant growth was not there. Living beings were not connected to the light constantly and desperately tried to maintain some balance and unity. At that time, the language was created to clear the confusion and it was reinforced by the collective mind. The collective mind was a parasite, an imbalance, that was created by the life forms on different planets. The life forms were able to connect to the collective mind and receive guidance that brought them further away from the planetary, collective growth.

Introduction

Earth was not affected by the schisms and imbalances in other planets and sub-planes and she was able to maintain the golden era. Earth's life forms were able to experience constant transformation becoming powerful creators and transmitters of the cosmic light. As there was no separation and schisms on Earth, living beings could exist in all layers of the planet. They could fly, go underwater, climb high mountains of crystals, teleporting to different parts including the inner Earth, being able to heal and transform their bodies instantly, communicate and create with their energy. These wonderful abilities supported the transmission of the cosmic light to all energy points in all grids and energy fields on the planet.

Wisdom of Thoth: Divisions in the new planes and Earth's golden era

While other planets in the new planes experienced schisms and separation, Earth was going through a high moment of growth where all creation was aligned with astral growth and the intention of the Source. Earth's life forms were able to exist in all layers of the planet. They could fly, go underwater, climb high mountains of crystals, teleporting to different parts including the inner Earth, being able to heal and transform their bodies instantly, communicate with the Earth's astral body and create with their energy.

Earth's creation shared many wondrous abilities to help them experience growth on the planet in the most perfect and powerful way. Earth's creation was connected to the high light that entered the astral body and the core of the physical body and spread to all creation so they can all grow in unity and grace.

Earth followed the intention of the Source but many other planets experienced a life of schisms. More sub-planes were created and new energy fields had to be produced to maintain communication between the sub-planes and the astral plane. The new energy fields were created to balance the low vibrations and supported the creation of the cosmic light bringing life to all creation.

Planets were able to heal schisms and regenerate themselves by receiving the cosmic light that was able to travel through Earth to the energy fields in the new planes. This led to several periods of growth to be followed by cycles of confusion;

planets were not always able to follow their path of growth as a whole being connecting to the high light of the source and other times the physical body could not experience an uninterrupted connection with the astral body which is a gateway to the cosmos and high light. Soon it will not be possible for these imbalances to remain confined in a single planet or sub-plane but they will spread and affect the growth in the new planes.

Introduction

Beings in the new planes have the ability to connect to the light of the creator and the astral plane. This is a cosmic law shared by the whole creation. All beings in the new planes have great capabilities to fight separation but the low vibration which is becoming constantly lower does not help them to grow and evolve. Due to the fragmentation on the new planes, astral growth cannot fully penetrate the physical existence and it is important that all energy fields are open to initiate.

Wisdom of Thoth: The purpose of the cosmic light

Some of you may want to know more about the cosmic light and what its purpose is. Before the creation of the new planes, the astral was a vast space of growth where all beings were created and remained there. The astral plane was the only opportunity for growth offered to the whole cosmic creation.

High creator gods have the ability to connect to the light of the source and create life.

Gods are not in control of this powerful creative force and they cannot reproduce it. Instead, the light creates through them. When the High Light passes information from the creation code to the gods' being, the form of a light being will be created in the astral plane.

All beings in the astral plane are in a process of accelerated growth, receiving and transmitting light, going through long transformations and experiencing unity with all life. In the astral plane, light beings do not suffer from imbalances, schisms or confusion; they are constantly growing because they remain connected to the light of the source.

Cosmic creation started to experience imbalances and schisms when the new planes were created. The cosmic light is an energy field that is connected to the light of the Source and its duty is to spread to the whole cosmic creation. Its special task is to bring light to the lower planes and connect them to the astral. The cosmic light offers beings in lower planes what they were able to achieve themselves in the golden era: unity, healing, growth, transformation and constant connection with the high creative powers.

Introduction

In this teaching, we learn that living beings on certain planets experienced extinction due to schisms and imbalances. The physical bodies were created to have the same growth opportunities as the astral body and to have an everlasting existence, in other words, immortality. However, when a physical body is affected by imbalances and schisms is not able to fully connect to the light and be part of the astral growth and cosmic unity. This can cause imbalances to grow and lead species to extinction.

Wisdom of Thoth: Extinction in the lower planes

Earth supported the new energy fields to be built in the lower planes as well as the movement of the cosmic light entering all living beings on all planets. This created a new layer of growth in the aura of living beings.

Earth was always at the highest vibrational state among all planets in the new planes and the guidance/support and light that was made available strengthened her connection with the astral plane and the intention of the Source. Earth did not experience any schisms at that time.

In the beginning, the new planes demonstrated unique growth opportunities, countless life forms with unique characteristics and many different vibrations. All these beings had a unique way to connect to the light and support life on the planet.

It came the time that something very unexpected happened: some of these beings in the lower sub-planes became extinct. This was a turning point in the process of growth in lower planes.

The physical body was created to have the same growth opportunities as the astral in a high vibrational environment. The physical body that carries a low vibration, is not in constant connection with the light and the cosmic unity, therefore, it will experience schisms and its reality will be distorted. The extinction of physical beings was a product of deep schisms and separation which did not allow nourishment, support and guidance to enter the physical being but also the physical being could not support and grow with other living beings. Extinction was experienced in many planets and this affected the growth of all planets.

Introduction

The extinction of beings will continue happening in the new planes and this will affect every living being including the elements. It will support a new planetary movement and the creation of new groupings in different sub-planes. New energy fields will be constantly created to support new growth and the effortless movement of the cosmic light.

Wisdom of Thoth: Separation and imbalances in the new planes

It became known that the new planes were going to become a breeding ground for imbalances and this will restrict their ability to connect to the astral plane in an effortless way. Furthermore, the astral and the physical body of a planet will experience a major separation and they will have to remain separate, having different vibrations.

The extinction of beings will continue happening and it will affect every living being on different planets including the elements and all creative forces. Planets will be physically moved to form new groupings in different sub-planes. New energy fields will be constantly created to support new growth and movement.

A time will come that planets will experience destruction and will have to go through many processes of transformation to create a new state of balance. During this time, a number of beings will experience a reality that is not a flow and a unity between all creation. This reality is separated from the cosmic truth and later will lead them to have consciousness.

An astral being does not experience a reality that is affected by thoughts, qualities, events and experiences; for an astral being there is only growth. An astral being does not experience restrictions and the individual growth in this present moment is a reflection of the collective cosmic growth.

Introduction

All our special tools and talents are stored in the body and they are waiting for us to be discovered. When you know your body, you understand that is a microcosm of high creation and a link to all life. Your body is your temple and path for growth and expansion to other realms. The imbalances in our physical body are caused by the lack of communication between the physical and astral body. This communication can be done by allowing your bodies to connect and regulate the light and energy that flows through them. It is important that you know your body not as a limitation but as your tool for growth.

Wisdom of Thoth: The perfection of the physical body

Describing life and growth in the new planes, you will be guided to see Earth as the crown chakra of a being that is going through an immense transformation, seeking to balance energies and position herself in the cosmic energy field. Earth is a highly active receiver and transmitter of light and the energy fields will allow the light to flow through other chakras.

The chakra system was created to support beings that are not pure light. The physical body was not created imperfect; there are countless opportunities of growth

and powerful gifts placed in the physical body. The physical body is a portal and its connection with the energy field makes it a stargate to the cosmos.
The astral beings of light will never experience imbalances. The physical body on the other hand was an experiment that needed the support of the astral existence to grow and reach perfection. When the light is restricted from entering the physical body, imbalances will be created and will expand to other physical bodies.

All this was happening on other planets in the new planets but Earth was still blooming, expanding and experiencing the high light of the cosmos. The imbalances made planets to disconnect even more from the astral plane and allow new subplanes to be created that carried low vibrational energy.

The gods' knew that more subplanes will be created that will have an even lower vibration and growth will be restricted even more. Life in the new planes is not guided by the processes in the astral plane; the divisions become greater and the schisms deeper. Schisms affect the connection between the new planes and the astral plane, the home of all beings; between different sub-planes, planets, the physical life on each planet as well as growth processes. Earth will remain in a high vibrational state until the new planes will start to collapse in order for new structures to be created.

CHAPTER V

Every plant and animal had a growth plan which was designed according to the laws of the cosmos as they manifest in the high realms. All creation was involved in their process of growth and they clearly understood transformation. It is important to understand that all beings are created to be unique and have their own evolution and cosmic purpose.

Introduction

The new planes were divided into an increasing number of subplanes and this created energy fields of various vibrations that restricted the flow of cosmic light. Low vibrational sub-planes affected the overall growth of the planets and the way they received and transmitted light. The communication between planets and the energy field that allowed collective growth constantly weakened and had to be rebuilt frequently.

The divisions and separation in the new planes planted the seeds of major imbalances that still affect Earth in the present time. Distortion, illusion, fear related to death and survival, lack, disease, pyramid structures, confusion, limited communication and light exchange are only some of the imbalances that will affect life in the new planes.

Wisdom of Thoth: Low vibrational sub-planes

The creation of the many subplanes created energy fields of various vibrations in the new planes. Low vibrational sub-planes affected the overall growth of the physicality of planets and their creation and the way they received and transmitted light. The communication between planets and the energy field that allowed collective growth constantly weakened and had to be rebuilt frequently.

Earth was not directly affected by the imbalances in other planets at this point; she was one of the creators of the energy fields that brought the cosmic light to the new planes. She was a creator, a healer, an architect and a carrier of great light, coming to her from the Source, reaching her astral existence, the core of her being and then traveling to all life that she created.

Earth was a goddess, able to connect directly to the Source and create but also spread her light to all life in the new planes. Earth's life could support life in the new planes if there were less diversity and a wide variety of laws of creation on different planets. The difference in vibration in the sub-planes created major schisms that will lead to the birth of distortion.

Introduction

The cosmic light brings life to the whole cosmic creation. When you connect to it, you connect to everything that exists. You are in communication with our Source and this communication can transform you, heal you and support your rebirth. The cosmic light enters your being and reaches all parts of your physical body as well as your aura and energies. All living beings can connect to the cosmic light. They can receive it when they accept that everything in the cosmos exists in unity. The purpose of the light is to spread to all planes and living beings to maintain life.

Wisdom of Thoth: Earth's perfection

Earth was able to receive high light and transmit it to the new planes because of the high energy field that surrounded her physical body and astral being. Earth's physical existence was fully connected to the astral. The whole being of Earth was astral in the physical in unity and they shared the same energy field. This was a perfect creation and the intention of the gods carrying the high light, the intention of our source.

Earth with her light, she was pulling all planets to reconnect to the astral plane balancing their physical and astral existence but this was not possible to be achieved and soon the physical bodies were affected by distorted energies. Their only connection to the astral plane was an energy field which was a mixture of light and distorted energies (similar to the aura of Earth in the present time). The physical beings that were created in those planes were also disconnected from the high light and were surrounded by distortion and imbalanced energies.

Introduction

In this teaching, we learn about the unique characteristics of the physical body created by Earth and other planets and what supported them or restricted them on their path to the golden era.

Wisdom of Thoth: The physical body in the golden era

Some of you may ask: what were the unique characteristics of the physical body of the living beings on other planets and how were they compared to the physicality of Earth's beings?

The physical body of Earth and her beings were fully grown and their transformation followed the overall transformation of Earth's being able to receive and transmit light and have an everlasting life cycle being part of the astral existence.

There was a greater variety of physical bodies regarding shape, colour, qualities and the way the elements were combined to create the physical body. In the high point of the golden era, Earth was able to create many more elements and this led to more complex physical bodies that carried many elements and had various qualities and gifts. Living beings were unique and it would be impossible to group them into categories; for example, there were beings who were a combination of animal and plant or fish, bird and mammal.

All these beings were multidimensional and had powerful energy fields that connected to Earth's field. They did not procreate, they did not feed on each other, they received light from their energy field and the physical body could create their nourishment. The physical body and energy field could regenerate and initiate all processes of growth and transformation.

During the golden era, Earth's physical body did not experience life as a third-dimensional reality. Living beings were aware that their energy field is part of the cosmic creation. They were able to experience cosmic growth through Earth's astral existence. They were aware of the guidance, intervention and creation of the gods. They knew that everything that they connect to is alive and is growing and transforming with them. They experienced Earth's body as another living being supporting their growth.

No other planet was able to experience a golden era like Earth. All planets, in the beginning, went through a similar growth and creation processes as Earth but this growth was often interrupted or restricted by imbalances and schisms. Most planets were not fully connected to the cosmic light and this created separation between the physical body and the astral existence.

The physical beings on other planets experienced schisms and the growth was affected by this. The unity between the physical and astral existence can support growth and create powerful energy fields that will unite the growth in the physical body with the growth in the astral plane and allow light to travel to all cosmic creation. The beings that existed on Earth were surrounded by these fields and the physical body was a pure and perfect extension of the energy field.

The planets in the new planes that experienced schisms were not able to create many elements that will be used for the growth of the planet and its living beings. Therefore the physical bodies will have fewer opportunities to grow, support life on the planet and nourish themselves. They were created to be receivers and transmitters of light but they were not given many opportunities to develop this vital ability.

Communication, nourishment, connection, creation, growth and transformation were all forms of exchanging light and the physical body was a light carrier. Other planets did not carry this form of growth and there was separation and distortion in the physical body.

Low vibration, schisms, sub-planes, imbalances created many separations between the different planets and physical beings. This was against the divine plan that wanted unity to be experienced by all life and the whole cosmic creation to grow as one being.

Introduction

The destruction of planets and sub-planes are the result of schisms and the inability of the physical body to grow and receive light effortlessly. The destruction will cause the birth of another major imbalance and this is fear for survival and death. These imbalances will grow and affect all planets including Earth.

Wisdom of Thoth: Fear and destruction

The great schisms in the new planes became wider and the creation of new sub-planes, reforming grids and creating new natural laws were not effective to protect and balance life. As a result, physical species, planets and whole sub-planes were destroyed.

Destruction gave birth to the fear of survival and later to the fear of death. Destruction and fear are never experienced in the astral plane. Astral beings are part of a vast multi-dimensional organism, the divine laboratory of life, that is fully equipped to offer nourishment and support to all beings to help them grow and stay in unity with the whole cosmos and the source.

Fear and destruction became imbalances that can only be experienced in the new planes and affected the physical body, the interaction/communication and the living experience of these beings.

These imbalances grew and affected many planets. It was clear that imbalances will continue to grow and eventually will affect all life in the new planes. Great upheaval and destruction are going to follow and this will affect Earth's growth too. What can be done about this? The creation of physical existence was a great gift and a new opportunity of growth for cosmic creation. But certain physical bodies (including planets) do not follow the laws of creation and creation is not anymore a balance and renewal act. Destruction was imminent and this will affect all living beings.

Introduction

When living beings started to live in fear, they disconnected from the process of effortless and constant growth. They experienced vulnerability and separation from the cosmic growth. Future destruction became a reality that they needed to deal with and this made living beings to create communities. The focus of these communities was the creation of protection mechanisms to help them survive.

Wisdom of Thoth: Communities of fear

When planets and sub-planes were destroyed, living beings received the distorted energies in their being and during a long period of transformation, they started living in fear instead of growth. The effortless transformation and expansion processes that were given as a gift to all living beings in the new planes, will be replaced by the fear of survival and the possibility of future destruction.

The beings who are affected by these imbalances, they will experience an illusionary reality that will affect all aspects of their existence. Their priority will be to protect themselves leading to the creation of communities and territories. In their communities, they will use energy to create protection, develop healing and transformation tools, work with the elements, and astral energies. They will master teleportation, raising their vibration, taking different physical forms, and will start building communities where all these abilities were taught.

All physical beings that were experiencing the imbalance of fear could join these communities and prepare themselves for the destruction that was coming. These communities were created in many planets that were experiencing schisms between the physical and the astral existence. Earth being a high vibrational being continued to grow as a mega organism of unique life forms and an abundance of resources and forms of nourishment to sustain and support life.

Introduction

You are here to receive the light and with it you will fight the low vibrational illusion of separation and polarity which has given birth to fear, greediness, survival and death of the real goal which is rebirth and transformation. We have the ability to create ourselves. We were given this ability by our Source. Without it, we will be non-existent. In the astral plane there is no death, there is no end. However, beings that lose their ability to create are non-existent.

Wisdom of Thoth: Survival mechanisms

Fear affected living beings on many planets. The destruction that already took place and led to the distinction of planets and sub-planes created schisms that affected living beings on different planets. This led them to the creation of communities and the development of technology that was focused on survival tactics.

The appearance of separate groups with their own ideas, beliefs and practices created the first signs of separation that would later lead to the creation of polarities;

beings started to compete with each other, going against each other and seeing the planet that created them as an enemy.

Their fear of survival made them create territories, use resources and energy to create protected areas that will help them survive or flee from a major disaster. Fear created competition, ownership, deeper schisms and separation from the effortless life of the golden era in the new planes. Beings are losing their connection with the light that created them and their life is affected and controlled by the fear of survival. This was the greatest schism that was going to affect growth in all-new planes including Earth. Soon Earth will have to deal with similar schisms that will bring separation reinforced by astral travelers colonizing and looting her resources.

Introduction

When one cannot connect to the energies of the planet and chooses to live an illusionary life guided by fear and the possibility of death is not a powerful being. Patterns of weakness and disease will be created and affect all processes of growth. Living beings who have lost their connection with the planet's physical and astral body will develop various needs and fears related to survival. They will fantasize that there is a far away land of opportunity that will give them the abundance that they need and all the time, they will experience weakness, hunger and disease.

Wisdom of Thoth: The path of fear

The energy of fear that started to take over the living beings in different planets remained with them for a very long time and affected different processes of their being. Living beings were not able to receive nourishment effortlessly just by experiencing unity with the intention of the Source. They limit themselves to experience suffering. The disease will start affecting your body.

The beings that experienced fear and survival lived a life of limitation. This new reality allowed imbalances to be created and many of their natural abilities and qualities were lost.

They allowed the deterioration of their being and the focus was on the creation of separate communities, technology and resources that will be beneficial to them in the near future.

Fear created illusionary aspects of the present moment that later will be identified as past and future. The present moment during the golden era was an experience of connection of all life in all planes. Beings receive all that is created in the cosmos and they use it for nourishment and growth and then they transmit in order to remain in a cosmic unity. When beings became territorial because of the fear of destruction, they soon planned to travel to other planets and create colonies.

Many planetary beings started to travel to different planets and part of the colonization was to loot, destroy and have wars with other planetary travelers. Wars and destruction were now caused by the same beings who were fearful and were trying to protect themselves from imminent destruction on their planet.

Introduction

The living beings that allowed fear to be their reality, will not be able to receive and transmit the high light of the gods, the intention of the source. They are not able to experience the processes that offer them eternal life. Instead, they experience suffering and disease affecting their physical body. The energy field that was created as an extension of the cosmic energy field, will also experience imbalances. If you live in a state of fear, the true power of your being to grow and create with the light becomes a forgotten memory. When this happens, you will accept everything that is presented to be good for you and you become addicted to artificiality and self-destruction.

Wisdom of Thoth: The journey of separation

When living beings disconnected from the physical/energy/ astral body of the planet that created them and allowed the fear of survival to shape their intention, life on different planets changed dramatically.

Their physical body transformed into a weak receiver and transmitter of light that for the first time was able to experience sensations such as hunger, tiredness, pain, confusion and at later stages, the fear of death. Living beings started their journey of separation and many beautiful gifts and abilities given to them did not remain in their new transformed body.

When life forms lost their ability to grow with the astral body that created them, the body created new sensory tools to help them survive. At that time aspects of the mind's functions were created to help them survive, overcome obstacles, create new ways of living and new technologies. The new abilities did not bring new growth; instead, their life became the starting point of a short life cycle with a final destination, death.

Introduction

The schisms in living beings weakened the physical body and their natural processes of growth. Certain parts of their body were replaced by organs with limited structures such as the brain, mind, ego and their duty was to fulfill needs, deal with persistent patterns of confusion, negativity and limitation. When people accept and experience division as well as the pyramid structure reward system, they exist in an illusionary state disconnected from the true purpose of all creation. Living a life of fear and confusion does not allow you to grow and fulfill your greatest task which is to become a perfect receiver and transmitter of the cosmic light and grow with the cosmos.

Wisdom of Thoth: The creation of the mind

The fear of survival that was experienced by beings on different planets, resulted in a transformation of their physical body and the loss of some of their physical gifts. They were replaced by organs with limited structures such as the brain, mind, ego and a physical body that was experiencing needs that were only fulfilled for a short time and then the body had to repeat certain healing and nourishing processes.

The constant need for short term fulfillment motivated life forms to create pyramid social structures. In these social structures the seeds of leadership, ownership, collecting and managing resources, colonialism, technology, healing methods and techniques started to grow.

All the above are signs of a lower density physical body, a body that cannot experience the cosmic growth effortlessly and needs to have a path that will lead it there. While life forms were transforming to low vibrational beings, the planets experienced energetic imbalances that affected their growth and creative ability. Furthermore, different lifeforms had different vibrations and different bodies and there were also locations with higher and lower energy. These imbalances created more schisms and led to the destruction of numerous planets.

Introduction

Beings that exist close to the Source were given the task to maintain life and create life through the cosmic light. In the cosmos, there is no superiority or inferiority; low and high positions of influence; possessions and power over other beings; ambitions, deceit, illusionary success or failure. In the cosmos there are no divisions; all beings are created to experience unity and their path is related to their essence and growth.

Wisdom of Thoth: Maintaining the golden era

Earth was experiencing waves of distortion coming from other planets and sub-planes, reaching her energy field. Her energy field was restructured to protect her from all distorted energies that were created in other planets and they had such a force, that were able to spread to many subplanes and affect life forms.

Earth was able to maintain the golden era. There was a unity that supported all life forms. They were all connected to Earth's physical and astral body and this allowed them to follow the cosmic laws. All beings experienced constant processes of transformation and growth; their reality was eternal life, abundance, constant connection with the high light, they were able to co-create with Earth and enjoy many gifts shared by cosmic beings. The light of the cosmos will renew their reality constantly in order to re-generate Earth's whole being.

Earth was connecting to the astral plane in order to maintain her position as part of the new planes but she was also observing that the vibration in the new planes was changing. The distortion in all its forms was rising in many planets and sub-planes and more schisms were going to take place. Earth had to safeguard her own creation and maintain her connection with the high light of the cosmos; the powerful creative force of cosmic creation.

Introduction

The destruction affected many planets and created a new natural law: the possibility of termination of the physical body, the end of a life cycle, destruction and death. Beings in different planets will experience a deep schism between themselves and the planet that created them. They will disconnect from the cosmos and experience a false individuality, leading to the possible termination of a lifetime. They will carry this burden and it will shape their lives and life on the planet. When living beings on different planets were not able to experience an effortless growth they went against each other and against their own being.

Wisdom of Thoth: The end of a life cycle

The planets that were created in the new planes could not sustain the high light of the cosmos and they experienced a separation between the physical and astral body. There were planets whose physical body was destroyed and this created a new natural law: the possibility of termination of the physical body, the end of a life cycle, destruction and death. This new law affected the purpose of each being and the unity that supported collective growth.

Beings will see themselves taking a path away from the planet and the cosmos and experience a false individuality, leading to possible termination of a lifetime. They will carry this burden and it will shape their lives and life on the planet. When beings on different planets were not able to experience life as an effortless growth supported by the creative forces, they went against each other and against their own being.

They created civilizations out of fear. They fought and colonized other planets because of their fear of death and their need to control. Some civilizations discovered a high vibrational planet and they started making plans of how they are going to enter its energy field and have access to all resources. Earth was the planet that became the trophy for many civilizations who were looking to escape the destiny of death while at the same time, they will loot, bring distortion, destruction and imbalances to the life of the planet.

Introduction

Waves of distortion will travel across the new planes and affect all life. These distorted energies will enter the physical body and energy field of living beings and will block the processes of growth and transformation. The distortion will affect the growth of the planets and sub-planes. Earth's energy field will also receive some of these distorted energies but they will not be able to affect the planet. The many layers of her energy field will create a great purifier force and will block all these energies from creating a cocoon of distortion around Earth whose ultimate goal will be to penetrate and block all processes of growth.

Wisdom of Earth: Distortion reaches Earth

The fear of survival, the schisms between the astral and the physical existence, the experience of death, the transformation of the physical body and its inability to constantly connect to the high light created distorted energies that grew and expanded throughout the new planes and became the aura or the electromagnetic fields of beings, planets and subplanes.

Waves of distortion will travel across the new planes and affect all life. Earth's energy field will also receive some of these distorted energies but they will not be able to affect the planet. The many layers of her energy field will create a great purifier force and will block all these energies from creating a cocoon of distortion around Earth whose ultimate goal will be to penetrate and block all processes of growth.

Life forms on other planets who were affected by the fear of survival will go against the creation processes on their planet. Instead of focussing on growth and their natural ability to support life, the fear of survival will turn them against cosmic creation and growth. Often they will be responsible for creating imbalances and fight each other for survival while polluting their planet.

When civilizations became aware that there is a planet in the new planes that distortion and death cannot affect its physical and astral body, they came to the conclusion that they can only experience a life of high light if they colonize this planet, connect to the high light and reset their physical body. This planet was Earth and it became a powerful magnet for travelers, intruders and warriors.

Introduction

All beings who are seeking truth should look at themselves and observe the many layers of distortion that were created in their being for many years. Fear, judgment, limitation, ignorance are not the natural qualities of a human being. They are impurities that were created by external forces. If beings did not experience distortion and fragmentation and were free to exist in a pure state, then they will have an effortless connection with their astral body. Distortion, fragmentation and illusion are three main reasons that can cause an astral paralysis. This is why many human beings exist in a hypnotic state far away from their purpose.

Wisdom of Thoth: Planetary destruction

The life forms that existed on different planets were affected by distorted energies that seem to become stronger and create multi-layered fields around them, their communities and the whole planet. The starting point of all this was the imbalances, schisms and destruction that was experienced on different planets, the prospect of the termination of physical life and the fear of survival. For many lifeforms in the new planes, this became their reality and driving force.

They accepted the possibility of destruction and death; it was brought into their whole being; it created trauma, negativity, limitation and an unnatural intention to bring/create destruction and death. The planets that they inhabited experienced energetic and physical imbalances, where the cosmic light was blocked and growth in all levels was restricted.

Life forms will be affected by these imbalances and will become part of the planetary non-growth. Self-destruction will be the next step. Lifeforms experienced many divisions within their being and the rest of the creation: the separation between energy and physicality, planetary and astral growth, the light of the cosmos and the light within, conscious and subconscious mind, cosmic growth and distorted intention. These divisions will grow more as the possibility of death becomes more real.

Introduction

The life forms on the planets experienced the powerful effect of fear, survival and distortion and allowed these impurities to shape their life and intention. They felt the need to escape, run away, protect themselves, colonize, own, destroy, fight, understand life as polarities and disconnect from their divine plan. They are going to use their mind to achieve the above and have the short-lived satisfaction that they are in control, winning the battle of survival.

Wisdom of Thoth: The battle for survival

Life forms were responsible for destruction on their planet using technology that was created to cause fear and death. Colonization was seen as a profitable way to maintain and support new technologies by gaining new resources. Other lifeforms saw colonization as the only way to survive and prolong their life.

The impure intention of lifeforms to travel to other planets and explore new possibilities of life brought waves of distortion. Their impure intention will travel to all planets as a form of distorted energy and open the path for them to enter their energy field. The energy of each being is a protection grid that maintains unity with the cosmos. When your energy field is affected by imbalances, the imbalances can spread to your whole being and affect all connections and processes of growth within and the environment.

Colonization was practiced by many lifeforms and became a powerful and versatile source of distortion that created multiple waves of separation and non-growth. Colonization allowed lifeforms to experience life on other planets, something that was unnatural and brought self-destruction to many of them. The next step was to focus on colonizing a high vibrational planet in the new planes and this was no other than Earth.

Introduction

We exist in a space of creation where there is constant transformation. We are here to support all beings in all planes and receive their support which comes to us as an effortless flow. We were given the gifts of truth, creation, freedom, expression, clarity, growth, renewal and rebirth. We are free to follow our path and all these gifts are the stepping stones. We can be free from fear and limitation; they are artificial products of distortion. We all exist as part of the cosmos that has many ropes and all these beings in all different planes are tied up and connected to it. There is a high light that comes from the source and flows through us, reaching all beings and all points of life in the cosmos. We are sending light to all beings in all planes. It is important that all beings are in a process of growth.

Wisdom of Thoth: The intention of Earth is growth

Earth received distorted energetic waves coming from other planets and spreading across the new planes. Her energy field was in a process of constant growth and regeneration which is an astral process of growth. It is the intention of the source that the cosmic light should constantly support energy fields.

Earth will continue to maintain a high state of growth and all her lifeforms experienced an astral-physical existence that was not shaped by the imbalance of death or destruction. Every moment was an experience of growth and expansion for all life-forms. They were all connected to Earth's physical and astral body and therefore they were able to exist in unity with all life on Earth.

This knowing/experience that was shared by all, supported high growth on planet Earth. The intense distortion that was spread on different planets and sub-planes created schisms between Earth and the other planets. A sub-plane was created to support Earth's growth and possibly other planets could enter when they will be totally purified and enter a state of pure cosmic growth.

Earth was able to experience the intention of the source: the physical body is in constant unity with the astral existence and both experience cosmic growth. The physical body was not created to be isolated; lost in a distorted space of imbalances; trying to survive imminent destruction; fighting for survival. The physical body can only grow and maintain its light when it exists in unity with the astral existence.

Introduction

The planetary travelers will travel to different planets looking for protection, resources, new technologies and new opportunities of growth. When they became aware of Earth's unique abilities to experience her path as a powerful creator and follow her divine plan, the planetary travelers became obsessed with the opportunity to explore the planet and experience high growth.

Wisdom of Thoth: Planetary travelers planning to land on Earth

Earth became the ultimate prize for the power-hungry planetary travelers. Their obsession increased as Earth's physical body continued to experience life as a unity with the astral body and was able to receive the high light and transmitted to all her creation so they can also be in a state of effortless growth. Earth was not affected by distortion and death and she continued to grow according to the intention of the source. The high light of the cosmos supported her growth and her being carried the divine plan.

The visions/ideas that were created in the mind of planetary travelers showed Earth as a treasure chest whose valuable content has the miraculous ability to be constantly multiplied.

Earth's resources, her high process of growth, her ability to receive light and exist in great abundance became the magnet that made planetary travelers attracted to Earth and kept looking for ways to land on the planet and make it their colony.

They knew that it was not going to be an easy task to experience life on Earth but many will try to achieve it even if they have to sacrifice themselves. Competition for illusionary rewards is another form of imbalance that will add its mark on the life and growth of the new planes.

Planetary travelers were involved with the creation of new technologies to help them create bridges between their living state and Earth's energy field. Their plans failed. There were lifeforms on certain planets that believed that all subplanes will be destroyed and Earth will be the seed for the rebirth of the new planes. Therefore all lifeforms who want to experience re-birth should enter the planet and make it the new home. Earth is a creator planet and will create a new physical body that exists in unity with the astral and follows cosmic laws.

Introduction

Do not allow the products of distortion to restrict your understanding of the cosmos. There are many different forms of life and they all exist in unity. They all receive and transmit light to each other. Your growth is a point of balance in this limitless creation of our source. Connecting to the Earth of the golden era, you experience the unity of all beings and the effortless life that is a flow that nourishes them all.

Wisdom of Thoth: Maintaining a pure state

Earth is a powerful creator and all beings that she creates are powerful receivers and transmitters of light and an extension of her being. All her creation experiences life that is not affected by fear, need or lack; life is an effortless process of growth when it is experienced as a gift for cosmic growth. When beings experience effortless life, they follow the intention of the source and they are able to receive and transmit without the fear of failure.

In this constant state, all beings, maintaining their pure state, co-create the collective growth which is also constant. Every single part in the creation of creation exists in unity with collective growth. Beings who have these experiences will never have thoughts; will never question their life experiences or try to escape in order to gain new power and abilities.

You may ask what happens to beings who are distorted; can they purify themselves and return back to their pure state? All beings have an eternal core that is constantly connected to astral growth and the intention of the source. Beings have to observe the layers of distortion on the surface of their existence and have the intention to experience the core of their being. The power of growth that exists in the core should spread to the whole being and create bridges or healing, re-birth and unity.

Introduction

Earth attracted different groups of planetary visitors and they all had different plans as to how to colonize the planet and control its resources. All these groups had different technologies and unique methods to help them reach Earth. Planetary visitors will focus on creating technology that will allow them to locate Earth and find ways to reach her energy being. All planetary travelers will persevere and they will eventually achieve to land on Earth.

Wisdom of Thoth: Plans to invade Earth

Earth was seen by planetary travelers as an ultimate prize, a new hope for growth and a way to defeat the fear of death and destruction. When living beings are affected by fear and survival patterns, they only see a limited and distorted part of the truth. They are not able to see Earth's growth, purpose and creation and tune into Earth's greatness by connecting to their own growth and path.

Similar patterns are followed by human beings on Earth in the present time: when they are not able to experience peace, growth and creation coming from their own being, they have no choice but to be affected by the fear and destruction patterns and become receivers and transmitters of distortion.

Planetary travelers started to make plans, create technology and invent new ways of destruction as the only means to enter Earth's atmosphere. Earth attracted different civilizations that had various ruling plans, technologies, purpose and intention. There were life forms whose vibration and experiences of growth were compatible with the ones that Earth beings were able to experience.

These beings connected to Earth's energies and the communication that they were able to create with Earth was their bridge that will lead them to a visit opportunity. Lower vibrational forms will focus on creating technology that will allow them to locate Earth and find ways to reach her energy being. All planetary travelers will persevere and they will eventually achieve to land on Earth.

Chapter VI

Earth in the golden era consisted of the most luscious landscapes with the most extraordinary variety of plants and animals, rocks and formations. All beings, animals and plants lived in harmony with each other and stayed connected to the energies of the planet. Earth was a planet of balance, harmony and abundance and an ideal home for high vibrational races that could appreciate her treasures and wish to enhance her beauty. Most visitors who arrived on the planet, tried to get all Earth's resources, kill and destroy animals and plants and alter Earth's natural laws; she is still suffering from people in control who try to constantly dismantle her and block her light.

Introduction

Earth was an astral being growing in the astral plane when she was given the opportunity to support life in the new planes and create a physical body. Earth and other light beings were chosen to create a physical body in the new planes and went through a process of intense preparation to enter the new planes and had countless powerful transformations to initiate the creation of their physical body. They were all given a divine plan that supported the creation and growth of their physical body as well as the collective growth of the new planes. Earth followed the divine plan and co-created with gods where other planets were affected by imbalances, experienced destruction.

Wisdom of Thoth: The divine plan for the new planes

Earth was a powerful creator where all life in her physical, energetic and astral body existed in constant unity, transformation and growth. Earth was a successful experiment of how a physical body can be created, grow, transform and stay connected to astral growth. She followed her divine plan and she was constantly rewarded for co-creating with the gods.

The physical body of Earth was able to experience astral growth, creating opportunities for all life on the planet. There were no divisions or schisms on Earth. The unity and collective growth on the planet was supported by a powerful energy field that was able to block distortion coming from the sub-planes and at the same time be a powerful magnet for the high light.

In the beginning, all planets followed the same growth processes. They were all connected to the light that supported the growth of their physical existence. Astral and physical bodies existed in unity and followed the same cosmic laws. During different processes of growth, certain planets experienced imbalances and this had to do with the creation of natural laws, the separation between the astral and the physical bodies, and the complex and intense processes of growth that created unique living beings on these planets.

The light of the cosmos can balance and heal schisms and imbalances but if there is no unity between the astral and the physical existence, the cosmic guidance and support will not reach the living being. In some cases, a whole planet had to be destroyed or moved to a sub-plane in order for transformation, healing and growth to take place.

Earth was aware that there is a divine plan and a high purpose related to the creation of the new planes and she will play an important part not only as a high creator and light bringer but also as a living being that will experience the distortion and imbalances. This was the only way for physical life to continue to exist. Earth would not abandon her ability to create life and her creation will remain in her space of growth and transformation.

Introduction

On each planet in the new planes there were different civilizations that occupied different parts of the planet. These civilizations were not affected by distortion in the same way. The groups of beings with lower light will experience an intense fear of survival followed by distorted beliefs and confusion. They will experience separation from the planet and its growth and this feeling of separation will expand to their relationship with each other and their whole being.

There were also civilizations with higher light who existed in the inner parts of the planet and they were able to develop an energetic communication with Earth's energy field.

Wisdom of Thoth: How did distortion affect planetary civilization

Groups of planetary travelers who wanted to connect to Earth's energy field developed a way to communicate with her energetically. They tuned into her energies and absorbed them into their own being and the being of their planet in order to accelerate growth.

There were civilizations on each planet that had a different understanding of life and distortion affected them in different ways. The civilizations with higher light were able to exist either in the core or inner parts of the planet or in the energetic field. They did not have the same physical body; most bodies could shapeshift according to the energy fields that surround it and their ability to carry these energies.

The civilizations with lower light, will experience the fear of survival very strongly in their everyday existence and often will follow distorted beliefs and diversions away from the path of effortless growth. They will experience separation from the planet and its growth and this feeling of separation will expand to their relationship with each other and their whole being.

They will have to create technologies to help them heal the different forms of separation and the schisms that they experience. They had an illusionary belief that their separation from the growth of the planet will allow them to have power and individual growth as they are colonizing different planets always aiming for the ultimate reward, landing on Earth.

Introduction

For many planetary travelers and civilizations on different planets, Earth was a powerful receiver and transmitter of cosmic light and through her the light spread to all living beings. She was a creator of high light and all planets remained connected to receive her light and guidance in order to fulfill their divine plan. Earth's high light attracted planetary travelers who were looking for opportunities to penetrate her energy field and land on her lands.

Wisdom of Thoth: The intention of the planetary travelers

Earth will receive and transmit light to all life in the new planes and will encourage connection, communication and growth to travel from Earth to other planets. This exchange encouraged energetic communication between the planets and the beings who were able to observe the energies of Earth coming into their beings.

For many Earth was a great creator of high light and they will remain open to receive her light and guidance. The multiple schisms that affected existence and growth in many sub-planes encouraged many civilizations to look for a new home. There were beings who tried to locate Earth but because of her high vibration, she could not be captured by their physical and energy body.

The beings who were able to communicate with her, were guided to the energy field and attempted to enter her physical body. They wanted to enter the core of the planet and experience Earth's greatness. Some groups wanted to explore Earth and decode her growth and creation patterns. Other groups wanted to make Earth their home and connect to the high light of the Gods, opening up to the intention of the Source. Earth will allow some groups of planetary travelers to enter her energy field. These beings were connected to Earth's energies and their entry was a process of growth and transformation.

Introduction

Beings from other planets experienced the distortion and fear of survival and death for a long time and as the fear grew it created imbalances and schisms in their being. In their attempt to survive and support their growth, they developed technologies to help them colonize other planets and get new resources. Earth being a powerful creator and light transmitter, experiencing the golden era, became the focus of many planetary travelers. Certain groups who carried high light were able to communicate and connect to Earth's energy field. This was the start of an intense exchange between living beings and Earth that led Earth to want to support life on the new planes by allowing certain lifeforms to enter her energy field.

Wisdom of Thoth: Planetary visitors enter Earth's energy field

Earth was aware of the distortion on other planets and wanted to safeguard life forms from extinction. She became aware that many lifeforms were able to receive and transmit light, transform and grow and she wanted to support them. These lifeforms wanted to enter Earth's being and become part of her golden era. They wanted to become an extension of Earth and create bridges for the light to be transmitted to subplanes.

Earth allowed some of these life forms to enter her energy field but soon she became aware that their entrance will bring some distortion that will affect vital growth processes. Distorted energies coming from the planetary visitors will weaken Earth's energy field and this will affect her ability to receive and transmit high light to all her creation. The lifeforms coming from other planets to Earth were not able to coexist in harmony with her creation. All beings on Earth exist in unity and experience life as an extension of her astral and physical body. They all grow with Earth and are created by her energies, elements and divine intention for creation.

The first visitors will try to connect to Earth's being and grow in order to receive the high light and experience the golden era. Certain lifeforms achieved to connect to Earth's energies and experience high growth. Others saw Earth's creation either as the enemy or the obstacle that blocked them from enjoying high growth. Other groups of visitors left the planet and came back with groups of lower vibrational beings, guiding them through the energy field and finally helping them land on Earth's physical body.

All these activities brought a lot of upheaval on Earth and were responsible for the end of the golden era.

Introduction

The distortion in the new planes and the arrival of the planetary visitors on Earth affected the effortless growth on the planet. Earth's ability to grow was supported by the unity between the physical, astral body and the cosmos. All living beings experienced the unity that existed on Earth. They were powerful receivers and transmitters of light supporting their own being and all Earth's creation.

Wisdom of Thoth: Distortion on Earth

The distortion in the new planes, the destruction of certain planets and sub-planes, the transformation of life forms into lower vibrational life, their fear of survival and their desperate need to gain power and colonize other planets and their landing on Earth bringing great upheaval, affected Earth's growth. The distortion started to affect many transformation and growth processes including a gradual separation from the astral plane and the high light of the cosmos and the beginning of a low vibrational experience that created schisms and distortion similar to other planets in the new planes.

The core of the Earth maintained the high light of her astral body but the outer layers became affected by the distortion that has entered Earth's high being. The planetary visitors will go against Earth's creation and fear will replace freedom. The unity that was experienced by Earth's creation will become distorted and schisms will start to appear. Separation and alienation will become apparent on Earth.

Lifeforms on Earth were free to co-exist and grow, connect to her astral body, feed on her light and the light of the cosmos. The new reality creates fear and separation between lifeforms: they exist in separate territories and have to protect themselves from intruders. They have to move constantly and many of Earth's lifeforms will enter the inner parts of the Earth where they can be free to experience the golden era.

Introduction

Earth was a powerful creator, she wanted all beings to have opportunities of growth and to be surrounded by resources to help them stay alive and grow. She had clear communication with her whole creation and one of her duties was to create the right circumstances for them to experience cosmic unity and receive light.

Everything that existed on Earth had to produce light and energy to support the planet's growth. The whole planet was united and went through purification and transformation as a whole being. They received light from the high realms and they transmitted light to support the new planes.

A planet of great growth is always attractive to many intruders. Will she be able to continue her creative work and not get distracted by visitors from other planets? Will it be wise to protect her creation and dismiss all those who are not part of the planet and want to create destruction? Earth was not aware of the destruction when she welcomed visitors. All destruction that took place on the planet brought great imbalances on Earth and the schism is still apparent.

Wisdom of Thoth: Schisms on Earth

Planetary visitors moved to different locations on the surface of the Earth admiring, observing, looting and destroying lifeforms. Many of them did not come to Earth to unite with Earth's light and experience a life of effortless growth. They came to destroy and create schisms on Earth. They carried with them the fear of survival and this is a weapon of destruction. Visitors destroyed in order to survive; this is their fight against their fear of death.

They moved to many different locations and their intention was to scan Earth's physical body, study the processes of growth and creation, explore the wealth and abundance on the planet and take with them whatever precious resources they could carry. Many planetary visitors did not want to remain on the planet and make it their home but they only wished to loot precious lifeforms and return to their base and then have the opportunity to return to Earth again whenever they wish to.

You may ask: how did the visitors create imbalances on Earth? During the golden era, all Earth's creation existed in unity and harmony. They were all part of Earth's being and supported the collective growth. There was no separation between Earth's physical and astral existence. The visitors were not aware that they were bringing destruction. They were not aware of Earth's golden era and how it was supported by the whole creation. They were not aware that everything that existed on Earth is a living being and if you try to remove it, the balance and the processes of growth are going to be interrupted. The only living beings they were able to see were the ones that had a form similar to them. Their plans and schemes went against Earth's growth and created vast schisms responsible for the end of the golden era.

Introduction

Earth in the golden era was a perfect creation and all beings, animals and plants lived in harmony with each other and stayed connected to the energies of the planet. Earth was a planet of balance, harmony and abundance and an ideal home for high vibrational races that could appreciate her treasures and wish to enhance her beauty. Most visitors who arrived on the planet tried to get all Earth's resources, kill and destroy animals and plants and alter Earth's natural laws; she is still suffering from people in control who try to constantly dismantle her and block her light.

If we want the planet to grow, we have to contribute to the overall growth of the whole being, Earth. This is a very important truth and can help you expand your consciousness. Our purpose is to help Earth transform to her first form, as she was in the golden era.

Wisdom of Thoth: Becoming aware of Earth's divine plan

When the planetary visitors landed on Earth were mesmerized by Earth's ability to grow and create. All life forms had access to the high energies in the core and the cosmic growth of the astral body whose vibration could be experienced by Earth's physicality.

The planetary visitors were not aware that everything that Earth created is a living organism and has the ability to grow and co-create with her. All her creation is sacred and cannot be divided or separated from Earth's being.

In the golden era, all life forms had a powerful aura which was a visible receiver and transmitter of the high light of Earth. The aura that surrounded all living forms was their tool of communication, creation and a point of unity. The processes of growth and creation on Earth resembled the same processes in the astral plane.

The golden era was the time where great light traveled to Earth from the cosmos and allowed her creation to have countless opportunities of growth. These opportunities of growth were supported by the light and existed in cosmic unity; they were all part of Earth's divine plan. When Earth was aware of her divine plan all creation experienced the divine plan.

Introduction

The planetary visitors were low vibrational beings who experienced life on planets that could not maintain unity and effortless growth. They were disconnected from the astral plane and the cosmic laws and every action or thought was based on survival. Their intention was to survive by capturing something that cannot connect to or fully embrace. Their imbalances restricted their natural ability to unite and co-exist and instead, they were led to a maze of confusion, entanglement with fear and destruction and then they were guided to a space of deep and painful separation.

They admired Earth's high light, they experienced its power but were not able to fully connect to it and receive the fruit of her creation.

Wisdom of Thoth: Separation on Earth

Earth's creation experienced destruction and separation when the planetary visitors came to Earth. The visitors were not able to exist in unity with Earth and her creation and support the collective growth on the planet even though they were given many opportunities to exist in a peaceful state, receive nourishment and become co-creators.

Earth was a living being of high light and all her creation experienced a life of abundance. When Earth allowed other life forms to enter her atmospheres, her intention was to offer the gift of abundance to them and teach them peace and effortless growth. Earth is a generous creator, a receiver and a transmitter of light able to create life and a perfect state for a living being to grow and fulfill their divine plan. She supported life on other planets because she followed the cosmic laws and astral creation where all life exists in unity and all life grows when they experience unity.

The planetary visitors were low vibrational beings who were disconnected from the astral plane and the cosmic laws. Their intention and imbalances restricted their natural ability to unite and co-exist so instead they were led to a maze of confusion, entanglement with fear and destruction and then were guided to a space of deep and painful separation. They admired Earth's high light, they experienced its power but were not able to fully connect to it and receive the fruit of her creation.

Introduction

When beings have a distorted mind, they have no clarity, have no connection to their true self. In this confused state, they cannot see their purpose; they are not aware of their path and ways to live an effortless life according to their divine plan. When many beings are affected by distortion they all exist in this space of confusion and they convince each other that this is a natural way to experience life. When beings

are finally able to see the truth, they will see distortion as a dark cloud that blocks their understanding and true abilities to grow.

Wisdom of Thoth: The mind cannot comprehend what the light can create

During the golden era, Earth's creation did not have the experience of death or the fear of survival. They did not experience imbalances and impurities in their physical body or energy field. They did not have a mind that can create separation between them and cosmic unity or effortless growth. Instead, they all experienced a deep connection with each other, Earth and the cosmos and this supported their ability to receive and transmit light and be in a constant state of growth and transformation.

When the planetary visitors arrived on Earth, they started experiencing the high light on the planet and the ways it can affect their whole being. They experienced instant regeneration of their physical body and energy field, shapeshifting to light forms and entering into a state of high light transformation. The planetary visitors tried to understand these experiences with their minds but they could not come to any conclusion. The mind could not comprehend what the light can create.

Planetary visitors will remain on Earth for a while, followed by many other groups who would like to study this existence and find ways to decode the mysteries of Earth's high light and growth. The minds of some of these groups arrived at this conclusion: if you are able to decode the mysteries, the wisdom and the power of others will become yours. The mind will continue: you need this power because you are fighting for survival, the end of your existence is imminent, death will always be a shadow that is dictating the way you experience your life.

Beings who experience this type of existence find it hard to coexist with the light and its greatness. They go against it. They are pulling everybody around them to go against it. This way the shadows remain in them and guide them to a path of self-destruction.

Introduction

Earth was created to be a perfect receiver and transmitter of cosmic light, a planet of creation, growth, healing and nourishment. All Earth's creation supported her growth and was given nourishment and healing to help them grow with Earth as receivers and transmitters of cosmic light.

In the golden Era, Earth was a planet of healing and high nutrition and all beings were fed with the high living energy of Earth and the cosmic light which brought eternal life.

There were many natural devices on Earth that were used to collect light and then it was shared with all creation. Earth enjoyed an abundance of cosmic light which helped her to create new species and develop a great range of nutrients to support their well-being and growth.

Wisdom of Thoth: Decoding Earth's Light

The planetary visitors were not able to decode the creation of the light on Earth. Earth created countless lifeforms, all unique in shape and abilities, great receivers and transmitters of light existing in unity, experiencing life on Earth in an effortless way that was not affected by the mind or the fear of survival. Earth creation went through multiple transformations and growth cycles that helped them to experience perfection and greatness constantly.

This was apparent to the planetary visitors and realized that they cannot co-exist with Earth's creation; they were not able to follow the cosmic laws and allow growth to regenerate and transform their being in full. This created a schism and was the start of a war between the planetary visitors and Earth's creation or against other planetary visitors who saw the planet as their own territory.

Earth created bridges to support newcomers transform in the high light. Her intention was to protect lifeforms and help them transform into receivers and transmitters of high light and spread the light to all subplanes. But this was never the intention of the planetary visitors; they came to satisfy their need for expansion and control.

Introduction

The planetary visitors coming from low vibrational sub-planes were impressed by the beauty and perfection they saw on Earth. Earth was a high vibrational being, a planet of balance, harmony and abundance and an ideal home for high vibrational beings to connect to the high light and grow with it. The planetary visitors traveled to many locations on the surface of the planet looking for unique and precious treasures that they can use to create new technologies.

Wisdom of Thoth: Earth's treasures

The planetary visitors spread in many locations on Earth searching for precious resources that will be used for developing new technologies to help them continue their colonization. Earth, being a high vibrational planet, should have unique treasures that can be snatched away and used in the production of new technologies that can control growth and terminate the fear of death.

Planetary visitors that came to Earth from low vibrational sub-planes were fantasizing about the planet for a long time; they were surprised that Earth and her creation followed cosmic laws that allowed them to grow effortlessly and in unity. All creation had an eternal existence. The planetary visitors were constantly surprised by what they observed on Earth and even though there was beauty and perfection wherever they looked, they could not integrate and follow the effortless existence that Earth's creation was able to experience.

They had a mind full of thoughts, plans and methods that will always disconnect them becoming one with Earth. Distortion was growing in them and was affecting their whole being. The high light of Earth did not find its way in them; it did not transform them to high beings of effortless growth. They were low vibrational beings looking for a gateway to eternity but they still carry death in them.

Introduction

The planetary travelers existed on the surface of the planet and were not able to enter the hollow Earth and experience life there. The light of the golden age is still apparent in the inner parts of the planet and all living beings that exist there are able to connect to high energies; this allows Earth to continue being a creator.

Many of you have reincarnated on Earth in order to connect to her energies and allow the cosmic light to heal the schisms. The human beings that are reincarnating on Earth right now are brought to create a bridge between the planet and the Source.

The bridge will be cemented by the cosmic light that is the extension of the Source and brings life to all beings in the cosmos. Unity brings life to all. This is why all parts of Earth need to be united and exchange energies of healing and growth; all beings should unite in order to start Earth's purification and transformation.

Human beings have to stop seeing Earth as a piece of land whose resources can be taken and used any way they please. They have to stop seeing themselves as the owners and rulers, supporting Earth's distortion. When humanity knows the truth about Earth and accepts that their purpose is to become receivers and transmitters of cosmic light then Earth will understand her purpose and this is to bring the light of the golden age to every part of her creation. You can help Earth when you are able to connect to your truth and allow your own purification to take place. When you receive the light it can become a creator.

Wisdom of Thoth: Traveling to the inner Earth

After some time of observation and planning, the planetary visitors started to cause upheaval and distortion on Earth. They followed their plan of removing living beings that they see as useful resources and gather them to a location in order to be examined and assessed.

Earth was a complex organism existing in multiple dimensions that were all co-existed simultaneously. Earth's creation was able to move from one dimension to another and this is how they were able to travel to the inner parts of the Earth. When a great wave of distortion started to affect life on the planet, many living beings traveled to the inner parts in order to protect themselves and their connection with Earth.

In the inner parts, they continued to grow and experience the light of the golden era. Earth did not allow the visitors to enter the inner parts and they felt trapped on the surface of the planet. The part of the Earth that they inhabited will go through a transformation and will experience separation from the inner parts.

Introduction

Earth was the creation of the Gods and their intention was to support her growth and guide her to become a high creator planet; the light that was given to her should grow and spread to the cosmos. During this time, creation took place in all parts of the planet and all beings were able to enter the inner parts of Earth.

The inner parts were created first and all resources, high energies and Earth's creative force still exist there. During the golden era, portals were created to allow living beings to enter the inner parts. When Earth experienced multiple colonization that brought destruction and distortion deep schisms brought separation. At that time, the portals kept a secret.

Wisdom of Thoth: Portals to inner Earth

The planetary visitors have remained on Earth and affected the growth on the surface of the planet bringing distortion, low vibrational energies and the fear of survival. Earth had to protect her creation and maintain the high light of the golden era and this led her to a powerful transformation.

Life on Earth was sucked inwards leaving the surface of the planet quite bare and almost lifeless. Earth's living beings who experienced life on the surface were allowed to enter the inner parts of the planet through portals that could not be detected by the planetary visitors.

This powerful transformation created new landscapes on the surface of the Earth. All resources and life moved in the inner parts towards the core of the Earth to continue with their growth as multidimensional and high vibrational beings. The light of the Earth in the golden era had high vibrational qualities and was used as a high vibrational tool. It allowed Earth to be a creator planet responsible for healing and nurturing as well as a pure channel for transmitting large quantities of high light to her own creation and the cosmos. This enabled her creation to exist in a high vibrational state and allow the cosmic light to create in them.

Earth was created to be a perfect receiver and transmitter of cosmic light, a planet of creation, growth, healing and nourishment. All Earth's creation supported her growth and was given nourishment and healing to help them grow with Earth as receivers and transmitters of cosmic light. The true power and greatness of Earth left the surface and moved into the inner parts.

Some visitors decided to leave the planet because they were afraid that destruction was imminent. Other groups of visitors decided to remain on Earth, hoping that they would find an entrance to the inner parts of the planet and continue experiencing the high light and the constant growth of the golden era. The groups that remained created various civilizations on the surface of the planet that went against each other and also fought against new visitors that wanted to land on Earth.

There was uncertainty about the new planes and their ability to maintain life as they were distancing themselves from the astral plane. The astral body of all planets was not part of the physical body; there was a continuous separation between them and additional energy fields had to be created to maintain some connection between them.

All planets were affected by distortion that blocked the cosmic light to enter their being. The cosmic light is a cosmic connection that all life shares in all planes. When a being cannot connect effortlessly to cosmic light, its growth is diminished; its ability to transmit and create with the light is also diminished. Many imbalances can be created when beings are not able to connect to the Light and then new bridges have to be built to support cosmic creation.

Introduction

Illusion can penetrate your being, pollute your mind and affect your everyday life. If you are aware of this, you are awake; you prepare yourself, going through a

purification process and then you focus on your path of truth. It is important for human beings to exist in a space of truth and growth and if they cannot enter a space of truth they have to create it.

Can you describe your space of truth? What does it consist of and what is your contribution to keep it alive? How can you unite with other beings in this space and make it expand? Human beings have to make decisions about their own lives and be creators of their own growth.

Wisdom of Thoth: What can you create with your light?

Earth went into a powerful transformation in order to safeguard her being and her creative forces. She allowed life forms to make a new home in the inner parts of her being and this way distortion will not affect the whole planet or its core. The golden era was experienced by all Earth beings in the inner parts and this brought balance and growth.

The surface of the Earth was left for the visitors to roam, looking for portals, creating communities, making wars or deciding to depart. The visitors that left on the planet hoped that new transformations would allow them to enter the core of the Earth and re-experience the golden era but they were not aware that all beings create with their energy.

If your energy is distorted, you create with distortion: if you have illusionary beliefs, you are fearful, sad, angry, disappointed, you blame others, you do not experience your true state and path, you have an illusionary understanding and experience of life and creation. This is a low vibrational state that will not guide you to the golden era.

Only when you purify and go through a rebirth, you will be able to experience high growth. Connecting to the cosmic light and purifying yourself are gifts you can give to others and together you can co-create this space of truth and high light. Healing and unity are necessary for the growth of all living beings. When you act with pure intention you are able to connect to your whole being and the Earth and start growing in unity.

Introduction

If you are able to connect to Earth and accept your purpose to become a receiver and transmitter of cosmic light in order to support growth then you will instantly connect to Earth's high light. You will achieve this because you have connected to truth and you have purified yourself from illusion and distortion. This is the purpose of all beings that exist on Earth. and united you should experience it in your everyday life.

Wisdom of Thoth: Planetary travelers build civilizations on Earth

The outer layers of Earth experienced conflicts, wars, destruction, death and destructive energetic changes. The planetary travelers who remained on the surface of the planet understood that they will achieve to connect to Earth's high light when they allow transformations to take place in their being.

There was a change in the beliefs and actions of beings who existed on the surface. For a long time, they aggressively demanded to enter the inner parts of the Earth and experience her light but the doors remained closed. Now it is the time to become one with Earth by cultivating a connection of trust and an exchange of energy that will become the first step towards re-opening the portals so all beings on Earth can experience the high light of the golden era.

For this to happen, Earth and all inhabitants need to connect to the cosmic light, purify themselves from all imbalances, transform into a new being and transmit the light of the cosmos to the planet and her creation.

If you are able to achieve this task which is a fundamental cosmic law then all fear, destruction, manipulation and pollution will disappear. There is no darkness when the sun shines; there are no imbalances when you complete a purification process; there is no fear when you know your purpose; there is no anxiety when you are creating truth and growth in others. Your being is the microcosm that affects the macrocosm; therefore you have to focus on its growth and start a process of purification.

The communities that were created by the planetary visitors became civilizations that spread to large areas and their purpose was to connect to Earth's energies and the golden era. The first communities that transformed into great civilizations on the surface of the planet, had as the main focus to cultivate and strengthen a pure, unconditional and continuous connection with Earth's light.

Their everyday lives, thoughts beliefs creation were structured around their connection with Earth, the elements and their energetic exchange between Earth and the cosmos. They opened themselves to receive the cosmic light and the guidance of the cosmos, purify from the distortion and be part of the transformation of the outer parts of the planet.

Introduction

The planetary visitors who remained on Earth carried in them the golden era and became the focus of their existence. They realized that only if they purify from the distorted energies of fear, greed, destruction and survival will be able to connect to the high light of the golden era. When a being can disconnect from limitation, connect to the cosmos and purify from distortion then he is walking the path that will lead him to experience Earth's golden age. If the planetary visitors achieve this, the outer layers of Earth will experience again the golden age.

Wisdom of Thoth: Earth planting seeds

The surface of the planet remained almost bare from animals and plants when the planetary visitors started to loot the lands and pollute the energy fields with their low vibration. They went into a desperate search to look for the secret portals and follow Earth's creation to the inner core but they did not succeed. This did not make them leave Earth but they had an awakening: they focused on connecting to Earth with gratitude and unconditional love and built bridges that could support future communication and common growth.

The new civilizations of the planetary visitors created a connection with Earth and she started to create or to plant seeds on the surface of the planet. During the golden era, Earth was created with the great power of a god creator. Her creation was powerful and effortless, transformative, and eternal and brought great peace and balance to the whole planet.

Earth could expand and create multiple layers of existence and at the same time, all beings were fully connected to her core and were aware of all growth that was happening on Earth at this present moment. When Earth's creation moved into the inner parts, she created only in the inner parts. She only knew how to create the golden era in a high vibrational space of growth, offering eternal existence to beings of high light.

The connection of Earth's energies with the new civilizations allowed Earth to make an offering: she planted seeds and the planetary travelers will be responsible for their growth. With this, she gave them an opportunity to become co-creators and practice growth, transformation and rebirth.

Introduction

The civilizations on the surface of the Earth dedicated their whole existence to connecting to goddess Earth the high creator and establishing a strong and effortless energy exchange. They developed several practices and sacred gatherings where they were able to connect to the high light of their being and use it as a tool to connect to Earth's high energies in the core. These processes initiated purification, growth and the development of new and powerful tools that will bring transformation on the surface of the Earth.

Wisdom of Thoth: Sacred gatherings and ceremonies

As most of Earth's creation moved to the inner parts of the planet, in order to continue with their growth being part of the golden era, the landscapes on the surface of the Earth changed. It was not luscious anymore; it was an empty space with very little life. This land became the visitors' home who were able to develop communication with Earth and be part of a new transformation on the planet.

These new societies and civilizations created practices that will enable them to stay connected to Earth and establish communication. This is the time where the first sacred gatherings or ceremonies were established. The priests/teachers will help all people stay focused on the practices that will support them to connect to Earth's energies and create bridges for these energies to move to the surface.

These civilizations scattered around the surface of the planet and one of their practices was to create vortexes of light to help them create openings to the inner parts of the Earth. These practices will become more powerful over time and the surface of the Earth will receive a new aura, a new layer of light. This is a sign that transformation will reach the surface of the Earth.

CHAPTER VII

Earth is able to create and maintain life and this is an ability that she carried with her from her golden era. We want to teach humanity about cosmic life and laws because this will help them disconnect from illusion and purify themselves. We want humanity to grow not as a parasite but as a cosmic creation on a planet that is going through a transformation. You can all support this by disconnecting from illusion and artificiality and connecting to the cosmos and the Source. We are all part of our Source's high light; we unite and support each other's growth that feeds the whole creation.

Introduction

If you wish to start walking towards a fulfilled life, you have to connect to Earth and start an energetic communication with her. She is a creator- planet and she can teach you how to be the creator of your own life and fulfill your purpose. Allow the natural laws to bring balance to your life and you will soon disconnect from the artificiality and illusion that exists around you.

If you are not able to get nourishment directly from Earth, you live a life of artificiality and you exist disconnected from her. Are you supporting people to grow? Are you able to receive and transmit light to humanity and Earth? Are you walking the path of truth and purpose, experiencing life on Earth as well as astral growth? This is a challenge for you; it is a challenge for humanity and Earth to fulfill their purpose and the coming of the Golden Era.

Wisdom of Thoth: The high light transforming Earth

Earth's communication with the new civilizations on the surface happened after long processes of purification and transformation. Both the planetary travelers and the surface of the planet experienced powerful and unexpected transformations that led to a new phase of growth. It demonstrated itself with powerful volcanic eruptions in many parts on the surface of the Earth, earthquakes and tidal waves that will bring purification and a new phase of growth.

The life that existed in the inner Earth will now find its way to the surface and will be the fertile land for new life forms to be created. All living beings that will appear on the surface of the planet are all part of the Earth's bodies, the physical and the astral.

Earth continued to create high growth in the inner parts; the golden era never ended. Both Earth's bodies, the astral and the physical were never separated. The schism was only experienced on the surface and now new opportunities were created for the schism to be healed.

The extreme phenomena that affected the surface of the Earth were a sign of new growth and the new civilizations were aware of this. These phenomena lasted for a whole cycle of evolution and brought new life that the inhabitants of the surface of the Earth had to safeguard.

Introduction

You can spend time observing the ocean, its colour, shape, movement and form, but you will not be able to see every single drop that exists in unity with countless other drops. You cannot distinguish one drop from the other because now they exist to form this ocean and allow the current to create the movement necessary for this creation.

When the planetary visitors are able to see themselves as part of Earth's growth and remain in constant unity with her, fragmentation, division and distortion on the surface of the planet will evaporate. When they see themselves as part of Earth's creation, they will not experience separation because Earth can nourish them and support their ability to become a perfect receiver and transmitter of light.

If all living beings understand and open up to Earth's energies, they will all be able to heal themselves and transform their being.

Wisdom of Thoth: Planetary visitors co-create with Earth

When Earth completed her cycle of evolution, she was ready to create a new landscape for the inhabitants of these parts. These inhabitants were the planetary visitors that a very long time ago traveled to Earth seeking the gift of the golden era.

The visitors remained on Earth and dedicated their existence to connect to the planet's creative force and once again to experience the golden era, the greatest gift. For their dedication and pure intention, they were rewarded with a major transformation. The surface of the Earth was transformed into fertile land. The new seeds were already growing, sharing the message of new life and new beginnings.

Once the elements of distortion and imbalance are removed, the precious flower of light and wisdom that the surface of Earth once was will be revealed and blossom. Earth will be reborn from within and enter a new cycle of growth.

The Earth of the Golden era was not affected by distortion and fragmentation and her purity and high light could offer one opportunity to all beings; growth that has no obstacles, limitation or boundaries. The inhabitants on Earth can grow and experience again a high state of creation and this can be achieved by purification and their ability to connect to the cosmic light, bring healing and clarity to Earth's whole being.

The visitors will not only co-exist with the new life but will safeguard, protect and nourish the new plants. They are becoming co-creators and demonstrate the importance of new life that eventually may lead them to the new golden era.

The visitors became agriculturists, herbalists, healers, architects, workers of the land. They wanted to co-create with Earth. This was the gift they were seeking and the gift was given to them. The new cycle of growth on the surface of the Earth brought new life and experiences for the inhabitants.

Introduction

Earth will go through many transformations in order to bring life and abundance to the outer parts of the planet. Earthquakes, volcanoes and tidal waves will bring purification and physical changes that could be seen by the planetary visitors. The new cycle of Earth's evolution brought many transformations on the landscape where water and land will constantly change shape; they will expand or contract according to the new energy field and the guidance from the inner parts.

Wisdom of Thoth: New landscapes on the surface of the Earth

During the new transformation on the surface of the planet, Earth's landscapes went through a number of big changes during new cycles of growth. The inhabitants will see water covering the dry land. Water formations such as oceans will cover big parts of the land; lakes and rivers will feed into the oceans and will be created overground and underground. Mountains will become portals to energy fields and high transmitters and receivers of light. Portals could also be found underwater.

Certain civilizations will live near the water and develop physical skills that allow them to go underwater and assist with the growth of life there. There were civilizations that will be established near the mountain portals and other groups will remain in the valleys and the great openings of the fertile lands.

These civilizations knew that many transformations are going to take place on Earth and were on the planet to witness and be part of Earth's creation. The new cycle of Earth's evolution brought many transformations on the landscape where water and land will constantly change shape; they will expand or contract according to the new energy field and the guidance from the inner parts.

The energies and life on the surface of the Earth had to tune into the energies of the physical/astral body of Earth so the surface can continue to be a living part of the planet.

Introduction

Earth is the creator of life. A creator gives unconditionally and supports growth and transformation. A creator develops her gifts when she becomes an open channel for unconditional love and high light. Earth is a gift and as a creator will shower her creation with gifts and unique abilities. Earth can provide for all her species not only food but also healing, purification, energy and resources in order to bring balance and harmony and encourage communication between all bodies.

Wisdom of Thoth: The gifts of Earth

The planetary visitors that have made Earth their home were given countless gifts and growth opportunities. They developed a pure intention to connect to Earth and her high light and she rewarded them with new transformations and connections.

At that time, Earth supported planetary visitors by giving them free will. When they first arrived on the planet, they brought fear, distortion, illusions, the fear of survival, the need to own, destroy and separate resources because they experience separation and schisms in their being.

Earth supported them to go inward and start their healing process. The visitors accepted the challenge and turned to Earth for support. They connected to her energies, her physical body. A powerful exchange happened when they allowed

Earth to enter their being and create in them; they became Earth beings.

The time came that Earth will shower them with gifts and rewards. They saw fertile lands, water formations, high mountains that were powerful receivers and transmitters of energies. They saw their home, the surface of the Earth transforming unexpectedly; they trusted all processes of growth, they experienced them in their being. They could observe life happening in the present moment and they experienced a new power that enabled them to nourish and protect as well as taste the fruit of life on Earth.

Introduction

The unity that exists in the cosmos is contained in the light of our creator and is spread to the creation through our creation code. Our unity with our creator is a high truth and when we are able to understand the wisdom, we will open ourselves to the possibility of being a creator.

Let's take our intention away from the outer planes which we always think as separate from us and responsible for our limitations. We are all part of the unseen, formless, all-contained, all-created power of our High Creator and we are going to start our quest to high truth and knowledge from this point inside us which unites and contains all: our creation code.

When you are able to connect to the higher parts of your being, you will be able to transform your existence on Earth, having more clarity and experience unity with the cosmos. You have to erase everything that blocks your growth. You do not do this with fear but with great happiness, seeing yourself free, healthy, able to connect to the cosmic light, allow it to heal you and also to transmit it to other beings. When you meditate, focus on the cosmic light going through you; this way you connect to the cosmos and the cosmic growth. Everything else is an illusion and should not occupy your mind.

When you have clarity, you will take the right decisions and you will be ready to move forward successfully. Do not act on impulse because often what you experience is not an expression of your true-self. Allow the cosmic light to go through you and see your impurities, blockages and imbalances leaving your body and make room for transformation and rebirth.

Wisdom of Thoth: Free will and healing process

Free will is an opportunity for growth. When beings are disconnected and experience schisms, free will can help them see their schisms and consciously start their healing process. Free will allows transformations to take place; beings can remove layers of impurities and step into their truth. They experience the freedom of leaving the old behind and entering a new cycle of growth.

Polarities are related to free will. Free will can become a limitation when beings constantly follow diversions, interrupt their healing process and allow the schisms and separation to deepen.

In your present time, free will is used by the illusion to create multiple paths, truths, choices, illusionary powers and limitations so people can remain constantly distracted and confused. Free will is becoming a toy in the hands of illusion leaving people empty from true guidance and fulfillment. The planetary visitors became aware that will only grow if they connect to Earth and be part of her cosmic creation. All beings are cosmic beings; they are all connected and can grow in unity.

Introduction

Observe a moment in your life that you were forced to act in a way that was destructive to yourself or others; you were being forced to act this way or accept certain actions from others and this has created a gap in you which can also be called a schism. You can heal yourself by starting to observe the schism and the distortion that feeds it. Create a space of peace in you and focus on your being and growth. See yourself as a seed that grows because its existence is only linked to transformation and growth.

Wisdom of Thoth: Unity will heal the schisms

Earth's intention was to bring unity to her whole being; to heal the schisms, and support the transformation of the planetary visitors in order for them to experience growth that will allow them to co-exist with the rest of her creation as one being. Earth's gift to the visitors was a confirmation that transformations and new cycles of growth have already started and they are going to continue as long as the visitors were fully connected to Earth and supported her creation.

The visitors or the "new humans" on Earth started to observe the birth and growth of the plants and all other formations that started to emerge. They saw Earth's body as their route to the high state of the golden era. What was growing on the surface had long roots into the inner parts where the golden era was still alive. Everything that was growing on Earth was worshiped by the new humans who tried to discover hidden powers, healing qualities and powerful creative forces. The surface of the Earth will transform and all beings will celebrate the new beginnings.

Introduction

The following teaching will share truths about life on the new planes. Were the planets in the new planes able to clear distortion and experience healing? What was their growth process and how could maintain contact with the cosmos? What were the new natural and cosmic laws?

Wisdom of Thoth: Rebirth in the new planes

While Earth was going through multiple processes of growth and rebirth, the new planes that now have transformed into planes of lower vibration kept expanding into several subplanes and their transformation supported their ability to remain alive.

Life in the new planes was restricted to limited growth, schisms and separation between the physical and the astral body as well as the cosmic creation.

The cosmic light and divine intention had to penetrate all these obstacles and create new seeds of cosmic light that will be planted and as they grow, they can create bridges for the light to enter all beings in the new planes. The creation of sub-planes was necessary but did not support physical beings to experience unity.

Planets continued to move to different subplanes and form new groupings that were not permanent. All planets wanted to receive and transmit light and move towards the high vibrational subplanes. Inhabitants of different planets were also moving to different planets to look for new life or resources that have a high vibration and can help them connect to the light of the cosmos.

Planets in the low sub-planes are becoming bare and experiencing destruction. Deep schisms in the energy fields are reflected on the physical body that can be torn apart and evaporate. The physical body of some planets was partly destroyed or it was divided into two or more physical bodies. The constant transformation, movement and destruction in the new planes will create new planetary and cosmic laws.

Introduction

The transformations that have been happening on Earth that brought new life on the outer parts were absolutely necessary in order to strengthen and expand the energies and golden era growth to the whole planet. This will bring stability on Earth and all living beings will have multiple opportunities of growth.

Wisdom of Thoth: Constant growth

Earth has been experiencing schisms even if the golden era was still alive in the inner parts of the planet. The energy of the golden era should not be restricted only to the inner core. This is going to affect Earth's ability to receive light and grow as a whole being.

Life in the new planes is affected by imbalances that have a parasitic attitude and want to transform and spread. The low vibration, the inability to receive light and grow, schisms and imbalances, planetary visitors moving to different planets spreading fear and the limitation of survival, the many sub-planes with their different vibration, the constant movement of planets and their possible destruction made the low planes a very separate existence from the rest of the cosmic creation.

The new planes became the low planes that have different laws and growth structures that can change at any time. After some time, the unique existence in the lower planes followed patterns that were recognized by the cosmic light which will assist with building energy fields, grids, communication and energy exchange.

Introduction

The astral plane is a complex electromagnetic field and its energy occupies the greatest part of the cosmic creation. It is divided into sub-levels that have different vibrations and growth. A simple way to explain this is that the lower sublevels are closer to the lower energetically planes of the cosmos including the Earth plane and the more you go higher the vibration changes and beings can move to these different levels when they are able to go through different growth cycles. Reincarnations are part of these cycles for beings that exist in the lower sublevels in the astral plane. The greatest space of the astral plane is its core where energy and cosmic creation is being produced. There are also sub-planes in the astral plane that have a higher vibration than the core and the beings that exist there are responsible for regulating or directing the process of cosmic creation, maintaining life in all planes.

Wisdom of Thoth: New cosmic law, reincarnation

Many beings that exist on the astral plane have as their duty to regulate the cosmic light and spread it to the whole creation as it is the intention of the Source. Certain astral beings were given the duty to regulate and help the light to be transmitted to the lower planes and support the creation of the gods. These beings will become guides or messengers and will connect to different planets or sub-planes and guide them to a space of growth.

This intense support from the astral plane will create new ways for the light to travel to the lower planes and allow planets to transmit the light in their plane. Growth was slow but it was apparent and many life forms focused on receiving the light and heal the schisms and imbalances.

New transformations took place that brought new opportunities of growth and a deeper connection between the astral and the new planes. This will open the door for more intervention from the astral plane. One of these interventions is the law of reincarnation where astral beings will be implanted on different planets, acquire a physical body and experience a life cycle there as a receiver and transmitter of light.

Introduction

When beings are totally disconnected from the cosmic light, they stop to exist in their current physical form. We all want to connect to the light of the cosmos and the light of our source. This is our purpose, to connect to this high light and transform. This is a very important cosmic law and affects every single being in all planes. You should be able to understand and recognize that your purpose is to connect to the cosmic light.

You should live your life to fulfill this purpose. You should connect to others to help them fulfill their purpose.

Collective growth always affects the growth of the single being to recognize its potential in connection with the whole. Collective growth is a great creator; all beings transform and build bridges between the limitless creation in the astral plane and life in all planes. When unity is experienced by all life, leading to growth and transformation, all beings can experience the intention of the source flowing through godly creation.

Wisdom of Thoth: Collective growth

The astral beings that supported the cosmic light entering the lower planes in order to initiate new forms of growth and transformation in all planets supported the creation of the Gods. There were times that the light of a god will take a form and communicate to the essence of all creation on a planet and other times the light of the gods will cover and travel to all sub planes where there is physical existence.

The gods will connect to all beings and balance their energies, support their inner energy fields and their connection with planetary and cosmic energy fields. Planetary laws should reflect the cosmic laws and all physical planets should share an energy field sharing light with each other and support the movement of the living light.

If there are beings who are totally disconnected from the cosmic light, will stop to exist in their current form. Collective growth always affects the growth of the single being to recognize its potential in connection with the whole. Collective growth is a great creator; all beings transform and build bridges between the limitless creation in the astral plane and life in all planes. When unity is experienced by all life, leading to growth and transformation, all beings can experience the intention of the source flowing through godly creation.

Introduction

In this teaching, we learn about the creation of a new cosmic law that will allow astral beings to connect to the astral body of a planet and become an extension of it by experiencing a physical existence. This opportunity will create a strong connection between the astral plane and the new planes, support planets and their creation by implanting powerful receivers and transmitters of light that have a physical body. These astral beings that incarnate on a planet will interact with all living beings and still be aware of their multidimensional existence and the purpose of this lifetime.

Wisdom of Thoth: Reincarnation, a new opportunity of growth

Certain astral beings that experienced life in the astral plane had a duty to support the new planes by regulating light flow, supporting processes of growth and purification. Astral beings supported the flow of energy in the planets' energy field, the connection between the physical and the astral body and helping with processes of healing and transformation.

The astral beings' role and contribution were invaluable for supporting the new planes to maintain a connection with the astral plane. This led to the creation of unique duty. They were called to enter the astral body of a planet and become its extension, taking a physical form and having a life cycle on a planet as a physical being. This new law that became common on all planets, was created to support life in the lower planes by bringing in powerful receivers and transmitters of light who will have the opportunity to heal schisms and initiate new processes of rebirth and regeneration.

The multiple schisms, destruction, the fear of death, the limitation of the physical body and its distant connection with the astral being of the planet created multiple layers of imbalances. Astral beings were called to bring the high light of the growth in all planets by taking a physical form and connecting physicality with astral existence.

The incarnation of an astral being will last for a certain time, there is no death but the physical body resolves when the purpose of this incarnation is fulfilled. The astral beings that acquired a physical body, can still experience their multidimensional existence.

Their physical body can change form if it is needed, and part of their purpose is to remain on the planet and heal the schisms. Often a group of astral beings will incarnate on the same planet at that moment and will have a common purpose or will support newcomers before the end of their incarnation cycle. They will coexist with other beings on the planet and will work with their energies.

Introduction

The new humans developed a strong communication with Earth to help them support the new life that started to appear on the surface of the planet. They experienced the plants and other living beings growing, supported by Earth's pure intention, unconditional love and creative powers. They opened up to Earth's energies, creative forces and gifts. They are becoming one with Earth.

Wisdom of Thoth: Astral beings support growth in the new planes

The new humans that made their home on the surface of the planet developed an intense communication with Earth. They exchanged healing, light and truths about natural and cosmic laws. These exchanges supported new connections and transformation in new human beings.

The new humans observed the plants and assisted them with their growth; they observed their effortless growth, experiencing the high energies of the core of the planet and their ability to receive and transmit light. The new humans connected to the elements and the energy fields of the planet and created arts that will support all life on the surface of the Earth. They learned to love, receive and transmit unconditionally.

Their purpose was to become one with the planet and allow the golden era to enter their being. Earth communicated with them that astral beings will enter her astral and physical body, they will acquire a physical form and co-exist with them on the surface.

The new humans waited with anticipation for this high moment of creation. This cosmic intervention was seen as the coming of a high leader, messiah, master, teacher that will bring the high light in all beings that exist on Earth. The astral beings came to Earth having a physical body and co-created with the new humans.

They taught them ways to cultivate the land, develop techniques and arts, transform and expand their civilizations and build an energy grid with Earth. They will unite with Earth when they connect energetically and exist in the same energy field. Astral beings will teach the new humans that Earth is their home and they will be responsible for the growth in the outer parts until the moment of complete connection.

Introduction

The incarnated astral beings will be able to travel to different parts of the planet, connect to the high energies of the Earth and communicate with the astral body, supporting energy fields and creating portals for high light to enter Earth's being.

They will observe life on Earth, the way living beings interact and create, the support they receive and in what way they contribute to Earth's growth.

Wisdom of Thoth: Astral beings incarnate on Earth

The astral beings that incarnated on Earth took different forms and observed the interaction of living beings with their environment. All plants and formations were created by Earth and the root of their creation was in the golden era in their inner parts. The new humans were called to unite with Earth's creation and start growing their own roots. The astral beings were able to take different forms and travel to all parts of the planet, communicate with the astral body of Earth and bring light to the surface from the core as well as the astral plane.

They were the powerful receivers and transmitters of cosmic light that were able to create points of energy exchange scattered around the surface of the Earth. The new humans will see transformations taking place on the surface and will hope that the golden era is being born and all parts will be united according to Earth's communication.

Other times, the astral beings will have a human form and will interact with the new humans. They will be their teachers and sometimes their leaders but they can only stay in this form for a while. The astral beings that incarnated on Earth were aware of their duty and purpose. They were receivers and transmitters of high light and taught the new humans to focus on connecting to Earth and the cosmos and become the bridge for high light to reach the surface of the Earth as well as her whole being.

Introduction

The incarnation of astral beings on different planets supported the growth of living beings and built bridges between the physical, astral and cosmic existence. Astral beings that reincarnated on Earth brought the golden age of the inner parts closer to the surface and all living beings were able to experience this high state of growth, absorb the energies of transformation and re-birth and transform. This was the time where large structures were built on Earth to receive and transmit energy and scattered in all locations on the planet that mirrored the connection points on the Earth's field.

Wisdom of Thoth: The creation of the pyramids

Astral beings continued to incarnate on Earth and other planets in the new planes. This intervention brought apparent transformation to the surface of the planet and to all living beings that existed there, including the new humans. All living beings developed the ability to receive and transmit light, their energy fields expanded and mirrored Earth's energy field.

Astral beings brought the golden age of the inner parts closer to the surface and all living beings were able to absorb the energies and transform themselves. This was the time when large receivers and transmitters of energy were created on the surface of the Earth and scattered in all locations that mirrored the connection points on the Earth's field.

Some of these structures had the shape of a pyramid and were created by different materials such as metals, crystals, stones that were found in underground locations. They resembled the natural formations that existed on Earth during the golden era and were powerful receivers and transmitters of light. Incarnated astral beings and new humans will build these structures using high energies that exist in the core of the Earth. The civilizations on Earth flourished and were happy to co-exist on a beautiful planet that shared with them countless gifts of growth and transformation.

Introduction

Astral beings incarnated in many planets to bring high light to all life and help them to continue growing effortlessly, being part of the cosmic creation. They were aware of their purpose, unique gifts and the functions of their physical body which enabled them to experience life on the planet, interact and create with other beings.

Their physical body was created by the planet using the elements but they had abilities that were unique, powerful, highly creative and were used to support creation and balance the unity of the astral and physical existence on the planet.

Wisdom of Thoth: The interaction of incarnated beings in the new planes

Astral beings incarnated in many planets in order to bring light and support the life of living beings. They have the physical body that will allow them to experience life on the planet, interact and create with other beings. They incarnated astral beings had certain characteristics, abilities and skills that were appropriate for fulfilling their path and exchange energy with other living beings.

Astral beings were aware of their purpose but were not always allowed to reveal it to others. Their physical body looked similar to other beings in their location but they had abilities that were unique, powerful, highly creative that were used to support creation and balance the unity of the astral and physical existence on Earth.

The arrival of astral beings was a beautiful gift to the living beings on the planet. It was a sign of protection, support and unity with the cosmos. The inhabitants of the planets saw the astral beings as the new leaders, teachers, creators and gods and supported them to remain in their location and focus on growth.

The fear of survival still existed in living beings but there was also an inner power and new clarity growing. The light brought to the lower planes by astral beings healed some of the schisms and created stronger connections between living beings, planets and the astral creation.

Introduction

The arrival of the astral beings incarnating on different planets, supported life and growth, brought light and unity and supported the re-grouping and the restructure of the sub-planes.

Wisdom of Thoth: The restructure of the sub-planes

The arrival of the astral beings incarnating on different planets, brought light and unity and supported the re-grouping and the restructure of the sub-planes. Planets who formed a certain sub-plane shared the same vibration and ability to grow. They received and transmitted light in a similar way and they also shared similar energy field structures and physical elements. Planets had opportunities to move to other sub-planes or new subplanes to be created to support the unique growth and light of a new group of planets.

It was necessary for astral beings to incarnate on different planets to support not only the individual but also the collective growth of all planets on a certain subplane. The cosmic light created strong bonds between the astral and physical existence of planets and brought a new balance. A number of sub-planes stopped to exist as planets received the high light and altered their vibration.

Some balance was experienced in most planets in the lower planes and astral beings continued to incarnate and support planets and their creations. Some of the schisms and imbalances remained but many bridges were built for the cosmic light to travel and many energy points became portals, stargates and unity points for all communications and forms of growth to strengthen and expand across the lower planes.

Introduction

The incarnation of astral beings will continue to take place and take different forms during the different growth cycles in the lower planes. Astral beings will be supported by astral guides to help them navigate through their incarnation and their important duties.

Wisdom of Thoth: New growth in the new planes

There are certain laws that have been followed by all planets from the beginning of the creation of the physical body. All living beings that grow on the planet, are part of the physical body of the planet, there is no separation and therefore they are all connected to the same astral body.

In the past, certain humanoid beings did not see themselves as part of the planet and were affected by the schisms of fear, destruction and distortion of death. They started to go against life, they experienced schisms and imbalances, they colonized other planets to find resources to fight death but instead, they brought distortion and fragmentation.

The invasion and colonization of planetary visitors affected the balance and growth of Earth and as a result the outer parts became desolate. New cycles of growth will bring some peace and stability and connect all life in lower planes to the light and the cosmic creation. Astral beings will incarnate repeatedly and will be supported by guides to help them fulfil their path and purpose as they experience life on different planets. At times astral beings will also incarnate in the core of the Earth to experience the golden era and in future lifetimes will bring the highlight of Earth to the surface.

Introduction

The following teaching explains the incarnation process of astral beings in the new planes. They are aware of the purpose, abilities, gifts and path when they are called to incarnate and also during their lifetime. They integrate with living beings and the planet, they support them grow, heal and exist in unity but they are also aware that this life time will come to end when they have fulfilled their purpose.

Wisdom of Thoth: The process of incarnation for astral beings in the new planes

The reincarnation process of astral beings on Earth and other planets can be explained here. The astral light or astral being will be called to incarnate and become aware of the purpose, conditions, physical body qualities/gifts and duties in the new plane. Part of the astral light will enter Earth's astral body and will go through a transformation that will create connections towards the astral existence (soul). After a number of transformations a light form compatible to Earth's light that can support the creation of a physical body will be created.

When this is achieved, the body will be created to support the purpose and path for this lifetime. At the end of a life cycle, their physical body will dissolve and the light of the being will return to the astral plane. During their lifetime they are always aware of their purpose, duty and path. They are also aware of the duration of their lifetime, the process within the physical body and being. The experience of the physical body and its energies become a unique part of their cosmic growth.

Astral beings are encouraged to incarnate many times and on different planets, taking different forms and have different duties, sometimes co-existing with humans and other times focussing on supporting other life forms such as plants, animals and other living beings.

CHAPTER VIII

When people exist in artificiality and distortion they are not fully connected to the natural or the cosmic laws. Instead they are connected to social mechanisms and rewards systems that encourage them to exist in a maze of confusion. If people were able to connect to their physical bodies, they will be able to heal every disease and also support the healing of others. Healing is a natural law. Your body has the ability to heal and renew itself. It also has the ability to connect to the cosmos and Earth for nourishment and healing

Introduction

Life in the new planes went through many cycles of growth and many opportunities were created for new life and balance. A very important turning point was about to happen in order to safeguard the existence of the new planes and for this new laws had to be created. Planets supported the existence of countless subplanes of such a wide range of growth and light and this created long term imbalances in the new planes. The new laws will bring more unity and connection between living beings and life will continue in the new planes.

Wisdom of Thoth: Unity in the new planes

New humans were able to connect to Earth and create technologies that will support Earth's creation to grow on the outer parts. The surface of the planet was colourful again. Many living beings such as plants, insects and amphibians appeared on the surface and slowly Earth allowed the creation of more living beings some of them coming to the surface from the inner core and others were new creations that supported the balance in the inner and the lower parts.

The volcanic activity, earthquakes and other phenomena, transformed the surface of the Earth into a new living being. This resulted in the creation of a new cycle of growth for the planet. This new cycle of growth brought connections between the outer and the inner parts, new energy fields and new natural laws.

Earth had to follow a new law: to lower her vibration in order to heal schisms and group with other planets. This was a necessary process for the collective growth in the new planes, the introduction of new groupings and the reduction of the ever-increasing number of subplanes. This initiated the creation of the galaxies and other star formations including the moons and the suns. The moons were supportive planetary bodies that assisted the physical planet in regulating its coexistence with other planets. The suns were portals of light and supported the physical and the astral body of the planets as well as the overall growth in the lower planes.

Many of the lower subplanes stopped to exist and the planets were grouped according to their vibration, light and their abilities to create and connect to the cosmic creation in other planes. Earth's lower vibration will bring new opportunities of growth and new creation.

Introduction

The new planes were going through a new phase of growth and will affect all planets. Earth will not exist separate from other living planets carrying the great light of creation but she will go through a process to help her adjust and unite with all living beings in all planes. All planets were able to experience the intention of our Source as a unified force and support life in the lower planes building bridges for the high light to enter, transform and regenerate.

Wisdom of Thoth: New planes, a unified force

In this new phase of growth, Earth will not exist separate from other living planets carrying the great light of creation but she will experience the same vibration, challenges, schisms and she will develop new healing and growth processes that will support not only her but all life in all planes.

All planets were able to experience the intention of our Source as a unified force and support life in the lower planes building bridges for the high light to enter, transform and regenerate. Earth saw the energies and creative forces of the golden era to exist mainly in the core of the planet and had less intensity.

Earth will move into a new period where schisms become duality and separation. Earth's creation will experience duality where humanoid beings create new civilizations that want to safeguard and own resources while Earth's landscapes are going through a transformation.

One of the polarities is the separation between animals and human beings both fighting for resources and territory. Animals and humans are going to be afraid of each other. At times that Earth went through many transformations that affect the climate, conditions of living and nourishment, animals and humans will fight for survival. Animals will be eaten by humans and vice versa, animals will be captured and parts of their body (for example their fleece or milk) will be used as nourishment. The body and the intention of living beings is changing: this is the time of survival.

Introduction

In the beginning of the creation of the new planes, Earth was the high light of the golden era and this high light carried by all living beings on the planet. Earth supported the growth in the new planes. She was a great receiver and transmitter of light, the crown chakra in the new planes. She existed on a separate sub-plane because of her high light and her powerful creative abilities. The planetary visitors entered Earth's body and created schisms that separated the inner from the outer parts. The incarnation of astral beings supported growth on Earth and other planets and created new cycles of growth.

The new law that was created to support the collective growth on the new planes expected Earth to lower her vibration and support the reduction of the subplanes.

Wisdom of Thoth: Polarities on Earth

The separation on Earth grew not only between humanoid beings and animals but also between Earth being a mother creator and her creation. Human beings will not focus on communicating with Earth and receive guidance. Earth's golden era was not part of their being; they did not see it as the purpose of their existence.

Fight for survival became an everyday experience and a constant fear. Humans and animals felt abandoned struggling to survive, trying to avoid death. The death of the physical body became a condition for living beings on Earth. During the process of death, the physical body will remain with Earth and the energy being will have to unite with the astral body of a planet that created this being.

So if planetary visitors remained on Earth and died there, their body will remain with Earth but their light will have to reunite with the astral being of the planet that created them. Some beings were able to reunite and others not. The ones who remained on Earth as nonphysical beings were the first low vibrational beings who are feeding from physical beings when they experience fear or survival. There were the first non-physical energy parasites that supported low vibrational existence on Earth.

Introduction

The low vibrational Earth saw major transformations in the physicality and energy field of her creation. Beings on the planet were not aware of their whole being, physicality and energy, instead, they restricted themselves to experience a survival-fear-limitation reality and saw their path as a series of obstacles and struggles all entangled with the fear of survival.

Wisdom of Thoth: Low vibrational Earth

Human bodies and energy fields went through major transformations. The physical body became weaker and more fragile. The energy field lost its ability to connect and communicate with all life in the lower planes. Humans were not able to create with or be aware of their whole being, physicality and energy, instead, they locked themselves in a survival-fear-limitation reality and were only aware of their fears and limitations.

The wonder of growth and unity with the high light of creation was not their daily experience. A limited reality creates a low vibration and a weak energy field which will support separation from the creator Earth whose purpose is to support and exist in unity with her creation.

When human beings are in a constant survival mode can allow the mind to be affected by deceit and manipulation. Thoughts and acts of manipulation carry distorted energies that can spread to the physical body and other beings and create a layer of distorted energy. This layer can grow into a pattern and many patterns can create a field or matrix.

When a great number of human beings experience distorted energies, they are all feeding into the matrix of illusion which is the home of all parasites such as low energies, distortion, separation, fear and limitation. Human beings will gradually enter more and more into this false reality and will forget about their true purpose being the carrier of light co-creating with Earth.

Introduction

Human beings have to stop seeing Earth as a piece of land whose resources can be taken and used any way they please. They have to stop seeing themselves as the owners and rulers, supporting Earth's distortion. When humanity knows the truth about Earth and accepts that their purpose is to become receivers and transmitters of cosmic light then Earth will understand her purpose and this is to bring the light of the golden age to every part of her creation. You can help Earth when you are able to connect to your truth and allow your own purification to take place. When you receive the light it can become a creator.

Wisdom of Thoth: The matrix of manipulation

Deception, manipulation, the anxiety of survival and the fear of death will become leading forces of separation in Earth beings. Even when humans created communities to protect themselves and prosper, individuals will use manipulation and deceit in order to protect their own interests against others. All these actions created patterns that carried distorted energies that shaped their lives and their creation.

Distorted energies affect the physical body and energy fields and create diseases. Diseases are patterns of distortion that remain in the physical body and energy field; they expand, transform, grow and try to take over the whole being and restrict its natural processes. The disease affects all parts of your being, it can create false perceptions, fear, pain and lock you into a state of limitation away from your true path. Diseases can affect individuals as well as whole social groups and the symptoms of the disease become the perceptions, beliefs, practices and lifestyle of all members of the group. Human beings have to experience a deep purification process, releasing these distorted energies and patterns from their being. Then they have to purify as a whole group, release collectively and experience collective growth.

Introduction

A distorted space is a space that is unclean, unpurified and the people who live there are affected by this pollution in the mind, body and energy.

When you are distorted you have no clarity, you have no connection to your true-self. In this confused state you cannot see your purpose; you cannot allow yourself to walk your path and live an effortless life according to your divine plan. When many people are affected by distortion they all exist in this space of confusion and they convince each other that this is a natural way to experience life on Earth. When you finally see truth, you will see distortion as a dark cloud that blocks your understanding. Opening up to the cosmic light, can help you blow this cloud away and heal the trauma, schisms and unpurified parts of your being. Purification will be the next phase of your growth.

Wisdom of Thoth: Purification

Humanoid beings on Earth built their cities in remote areas either underground, in caves, in thick forests, or on mountain openings. These cities gradually expanded and followed intricate designs with multiple communal and private spaces, decorated with Earth's treasures like crystals, sacred waters, stones and other resources from the depths of the Earth.

While most groups lived in fear and survival, there were other groups that focussed on reconnecting to Earth and bringing to the surface the high growth of the golden era. The members of these groups can be seen forming a devoted priesthood, mystery school, sacred space of purification and connection to Earth and the high light.

Often these groups lived isolated, focusing on purifying themselves and maintaining a connection with the powerful creative forces in the cosmos. Sometimes, they will mix with other groups in order to bring the new practices to people who are suffering from disease and will become an important part of this civilization. Disease will shape communities; disease will never go, it will expand and grow and create a new path for humanoid beings: the path of death.

Wisdom of Thoth: Disease and Death

Disease and death brought distortion in the being. Distortion has many different effects in a being and it is important to observe it. Distortion can appear as a dark cloud blocking you from experiencing a life of truth but it can also become a state; in this case, you experience distortion with your whole being. When this happens, you are unconscious of the natural processes within your body and energy field, you experience a deep and profound hypnotic state.

There is a veil of deep confusion separating you from your true purpose and in this hypnotic state, you are guided to experience life with your mind which can become a generator of fear, negativity and limitation. When this happens, your reality is not your truth; there is an illusionary reality that is created in your mind and is supported by other people who also experience a distorted reality.

People are convinced that life is a struggle and it is natural to feel lost or unhappy. Having pain, disease, trauma can be a common experience in your reality. Distortion does not bring acceptance, it brings divisions and polarities. The confused mind becomes a negative mind. Negativity is about the fight between right and wrong, blaming and judging, competition and the fear of losing, vulnerability and limitations, ego behavior that is fuelled by the fear of survival. Distortion is not a living being but it feeds from people's energy. It can grow and expand when many people are affected by it and experience the same distorted reality. In the present moment, human beings experience a global distortion that affects people in different locations on the surface of the Earth. They all experience the same fear patterns and similar hypnotic state focussing on survival, disease and death.

Introduction

Living a life of emptiness and confusion does not allow you to grow and fulfil your greatest task which is to become a perfect receiver and transmitter of the cosmic light and heal humanity and Earth. Perhaps some of you believe that your purpose is to reach the top levels of the pyramid; the higher you can get the better or follow the social expectations and the short lived satisfaction.

Currently, people on Earth are trapped in a low vibrational reality because of the high level of distortion. Imbalances appear in all expressions of their lives and they are unable to heal themselves because they are unaware of their true state. Ignorance and confusion will not lead you to harmony and fulfilment. You have to be pure and true to your calling and purpose.

Wisdom of Thoth: How does distortion affect your being?

Distortion brings separation within your being. You perceive reality as a picture cut in multiple pieces and scattered away. You have to look for all the pieces and even if you find one it is not enough, it does not enable you to see the whole picture. You continue with your search, you get more pieces but they do not fit with each other and you discard them.

The separation that is a product of distortion has created a deep schism that caused the division of masculine and feminine. Before humanoid beings experience physical characteristics of masculinity or femininity, they experience the separation of feminine and masculine in their energy field.

Like any other separation or schisms, at first, it will appear as an impurity. Impurities are caused by distortion and the work of the distortion is supported by low vibration and limited growth.

When beings cannot see themselves as one with all life, when they are not able to experience cosmic unity that is an eternal mechanism for growth, then distortion, separation, impurities, divisions start to appear. Fear is an impurity that can affect your energetic field, physical body and perception.

When impurities grow within the energetic field of a being, they already create schisms within the field. This affects its ability to regenerate itself, receive and transmit light, expand and unite with the greater energy fields of the Earth and the cosmos. Multiple schisms in your energy body will affect the physical body and mind. The physical body will experience diseases and the mind will experience distorted realities. This is how the polarities of masculine and feminine were created on Earth.

Introduction

You have to look for peace within you and accept everything that you are including the schisms that you need to heal. People who need healing will receive cosmic light in great abundance. Being in a state of peace and acceptance, connecting to everything that was created in you in this lifetime and opening up to receive healing, will help you experience a strong connection to the cosmos.

If you focus on fear and limitation then you are going to experience the opposite effect; the schism will grow. Destruction is not a natural state for any being. Therefore you are responsible for bringing peace in you and to other beings around you This can be done by releasing the fear and limitation that you have experienced in the past.

Your purity is your weapon and this weapon can only bring growth.

Wisdom of Thoth: Unity, healing, purity

In the golden era all beings existed in unity. They experienced the unified energy field and the physical body was part of Earth's body. They did not perceive their being as a separate unit but they were able to grow, receive and transmit light as a part of the Earth-being.

This is a high state of existence and allows the unity of all life to experience cosmic growth and be in constant expansion. The high existence is supported by the high light of the cosmos entering all beings and regenerating all life on Earth. The growth that Earth experiences in the core of her being can also be experienced in the outer parts. There is no separation, impurities, or distortion when life is experienced as a sacred unity.

For the human beings who wish to heal themselves, they have to restore unity within their being. Become aware of all elements that form your being and experience the way they grow; experience your being's potential to grow in unity with all life. This is a powerful state to start your healing process. In this state, you will heal polarities, divisions impurities and see yourself as a diaphanous being connected to Earth's core. A diaphanous being has no impurities or limitations; it is an open channel and effortlessly receives and transmits the light of the cosmos and the Earth's energies. A diaphanous being allows expansion and unity to create its state of existence.

Introduction

Unity brings life to all. This is why all parts of Earth need to be united and exchange energies of healing and growth; all beings should unite in order to start Earth's purification and transformation.

Human beings have to stop seeing themselves as the owners and rulers and instead connect to Earth's essence and grow with her. When humanity knows the truth about Earth and accepts that their purpose is to become receivers and transmitters of cosmic light then Earth will understand her purpose and this is to bring the light of the golden age to every part of her creation. You can help Earth when you are able to connect to your truth and allow your own purification to take place. When you receive the light it can become a creator.

Wisdom of Thoth: Unity and growth on Earth

In the golden era, all beings, the physical and astral being Earth were unified into one eternal being of constant transformation and growth. There was no separation between the astral and the physical body of Earth as the one gave birth to the other and Earth's living creation was part of the Earth's body. All living beings followed the same processes of growth and were all experienced at the present moment.

Growth was supported by Earth's energy field which was able to connect to the astral plane and receive the cosmic light, the high creative force, in abundance. The physical existence was a rewarding path, and beings were able to carry gifts in their physical body, energy and astral existence. This high moment of creation on Earth should be known and experienced by all human beings at all times. Earth's golden era is in all of you who are connecting to Earth right now. She will guide you, she will show you the golden era in her body and energy field and you will need to know nothing more.

When this high truth becomes your truth, all distortion will be erased and fear will be healed. You are a powerful being, a co-creator with Earth, the experience of the golden era is a gift that you hold and you will learn to offer it to others without hesitation. You become the golden river that will lead humanity to the golden land.

Introduction

All beings have a unique path and the astral plane is created to offer countless growth opportunities. Other times your reincarnation depends on your connection with your spirit guides. They are the ones who provide you with a life plan and clarify your purpose and tools. Freedom means that you are not attached to a certain persona including your masculine or feminine attributes. Where there is opposition there is also separation and fragmentation and the purpose of all beings is unity.

Wisdom of Thoth: The schism of masculine and feminine

Some of you may want to know about the schism of masculine and feminine energies and the creation of the feminine and masculine physical bodies. In the golden era Earth's energy field was supported and nourished by the cosmic light, the high light of the Gods-Creators and the light of Earth's astral body.

Earth's energy field reflected the perfection of the astral energy field which is in constant growth and transformation because all bodies are transforming at the same time. In the astral plane, light beings or energies are not divided into masculine or feminine; divisions, schisms or polarities do not exist in the higher planes because they are an obstacle to unification and growth.

When planetary visitors landed on Earth, they brought with them their distorted mind, their polluted body and their fragmented energy field. Everything that they brought with them did not match Earth's energy so these beings became a living schism affecting the planet's processes of growth.

When Earth's creation left the upper parts and moved inwards, a schism on Earth's body and energy field was created. This impurity was the seed that gave life to all schisms that affected the planet and her creation through all cycles of growth. Earth was not able to restore her high light and direct connection with the high light. She was not able to restore the golden era in her whole being and reunite all her bodies. This schism is still affecting Earth's growth.

Introduction

Living beings will experience the duality and separation of the masculine and the feminine in their energy field. It will appear as an impurity, distorted pattern or imbalance and affect their energy field and the physical body. When the imbalance of masculine and feminine became permanent, it started to define them. In future life cycles, more beings will carry these imbalances and masculine and feminine becomes will become an archetype and a pattern on the physical body.

Wisdom of Thoth: Defining masculine and feminine

The new humans remained on Earth and experienced many cycles of growth. At the end of the golden era they had to go through many transformations to allow them to connect to the golden era and re-experience high growth. Their transformation supported their connection and communication with Earth and they remained on the planet to experience many cycles of growth.

The schisms remained and as Earth experienced a low vibration, the feminine and masculine characteristics started to emerge.

Masculinity and femininity were parts of a whole that were removed or started to experience life as a separate entity. These divisions are the branches of a deeper division that brings separation between the inner and outer parts of the planet.

Organisms will experience the duality of the masculine and the feminine in their energy field and then will appear as an impurity, distorted pattern or imbalance and affect their body. In the beginning, beings carried this imbalance and as it became permanent, it started to define them. In future life cycles, more beings will carry these imbalances and masculine and feminine becomes more defined, it becomes an archetype and a pattern on the physical body.

Introduction

In lower planes, separation and polarity are apparent and are often viewed as natural laws. You understand yourselves as being a single unit of physicality and energy that came to Earth to exist and function as one single being. This is happening because transformation and growth are not constant.

Your understanding of higher planes and the beings that exist there are related to what you experience in your reality. You accept a masculine or feminine god with a physical form that is surrounded by physical objects or Earth-like nature. You imagine that high beings have technology and physical needs as well as personality and character.

The high gods of the Pleroma are a unity that is able to connect to the source and bring its light to the cosmos. They cannot be seen or touched; I can simply describe them as an unseen electromagnetic field whose purpose is to create. This electromagnetic field does not experience creation by expanding but by connecting to the cosmos and transmitting light to it in order for the cosmos to expand.

New humans experience a powerful division in their being that demonstrates the importance or lack of growth, transformation, rebirth, connecting to Earth and her creation sharing light and healing. The feminine energies point to the lack of growth and guide beings to experience Earth's path.

Wisdom of Thoth: Feminine energy

The first division that was created was the feminine energy. New humans experience a powerful division in their being that demonstrates the importance or lack of growth, transformation, rebirth, connecting to Earth and her creation sharing light and healing. The feminine energies point to the lack of growth and guide beings to experience Earth's path.

Many beings carried the feminine energies and allowed them to transform their physical body and perception. Earth went through a number of cycles of growth and the feminine energies were not purified but they became a deeper division in human beings, animals and plants that existed on the outer parts of the planet. They affected the growth of the physical body; new limitations and impurities will create the feminine element in the body.

All beings were focusing on achieving the feminine characteristics in their body and energy. During this time, Earth's creation on the surface will experience the first polarity: feminine vs masculine. If your body and energy is not able to transform into feminine, different limitations and impurities will create a weaker form: the masculine. The first polarity that was experienced by all beings on the surface of the Earth led to more division and separations: the rulers of civilizations should be a feminine being and the masculine are the workers or the servants that had to obey. At this time social pyramid structures were developed and beings will take a social position according to their feminine or masculine form.

The social pyramid structure supported or created divisions within the feminine and the masculine. The mind will have to invent why these divisions are acceptable and how they can support humanity as a whole. The mind will become a receiver of distortion and the creator of stories of judgement, defence, expection, argument, reasoning, explanation and logic.

Introduction

Manipulation and everything that is related to it is the power of the weak. There are people on your planet who want the title of a god and their twisted minds have invented manipulation and destruction systems as a way to become a god. I know that on Earth there are people who control minds and bodies but this happens because you let them control you. You are working too hard to support the illusion that was given to you as reality and you are too exhausted to see the truth. Truth is hard to find when you support illusion. You have to be brave and cut the ties that connect you to false realities. You have to remember that illusion takes many forms and often presents itself as a need for survival.

Wisdom of Thoth: The new rulers

The feminine beings became rulers and with the masculine beings created the social pyramid structure. They all thought that this would be a great system that will help them create powerful civilizations on Earth. Their mind developed the technique of logic to justify the multiple schisms and impurities of the new system. Human beings used the pyramid system in every aspect of their lives.

Every living existence had to be labelled and placed on the pyramid. Therefore the mind had to create ideas, beliefs, explanations, titles and labels for every being and natural phenomenon on the surface of the Earth. Logic was a mind process that will be developed in order to support the new systems.

Human beings are not connecting or communicating with Earth and the opportunity to re-experience the golden era and unify all parts of the planet starts to evaporate. Human beings will experience more schisms: experiencing life on Earth as eternal beings without having the fear and limitation will change to having a lifetime that will come to an end.

The life cycles of the beings on Earth were long (many hundreds of years old) and over a long period of time, they started to get shorter. Schisms can only create more imbalances and further schisms and the time came that the feminine was no longer seen as superior; the masculine will take the role of the leader. Astral beings will continue incarnating on Earth and their physical body will adopt the characteristics of the masculine and feminine and their life experience on Earth was to inherit a mind, body and energy that will have to heal and reconnect to Earth.

Epilogue

The time has come that the living beings on Earth should know about Earth's divine plan, her cycles of growth, her transformations and all divine intervention that supported her to birth her physical body and create the golden era. Earth's golden era is not a fantasy or an illusion but a long period of high growth where Earth was able to unite astral and physical existence and give to both of them the opportunity to grow like branches on the same tree.

The golden era is a great lesson for creators, human beings who seek the light in them, for the new communities that they are going to build on Earth and all creation processes that will bring the new paradigm. The high growth of the golden era can be achieved by all human beings; it is the effortless flow, the gift of unity, coexistence with Earth and all life in all planes, the countless opportunities of growth and the inner bliss that human beings can experience when they follow their path and fulfill their purpose.

All human beings are creators of the golden era and right now they have a major opportunity to bring the golden era on Earth into their being and their communities. Invite the light of the golden era in all everyday activities. When you talk to people, you should talk to them about the golden era, when you want to support or heal them you share the light and unconditional love of the golden era, when you build communities, you create the golden era and you make it accessible for all people to join and experience growth there. You learn to give, share, coexist, live a life of orgasmic bliss, be able to see the countless opportunities and experience them in the most direct and effortless way. True fulfilment becomes a fruit that is hanging on a tree in front of you, stretch your arm and you will have the fruit in your hand.

Golden era is empowerment. You start observing yourself, empower your physical body and have a direct connection with the light and the physical body. You are going to learn that all physical bodies can grow in unity and your body is tuned to all physical life on Earth. When you experience imbalances in your body, you know that distortion is affecting other bodies on Earth at this present moment. Then you have to look for the golden era: you connect to the high receivers and transmitters of light on Earth, the plants, elements, animals, Earth's core energies and you create a portal for the high light of the golden era to enter your physical body. All human beings who have reincarnated on Earth at this time are called to create bridges for the light of the golden era to reach every living being, energy point, intention, breath, truth and path so new transformations can take place.

The golden era should rise from the depths of Earth's core and become an ocean of opportunity for all beings on Earth. The fear, limitation, illusion and self-harm that people experience on Earth they are pebbles and in front of you there is this vast ocean, the golden era. Do not focus on the obstacle, focus on the greatness and dedicate your life to create, express, share, grow and heal with greatness.

-Thoth-

DIALOGUE WITH THOTH

We received several questions from order members and students and below we present a dialogue be

Question

Have low beings a purpose on Earth? Why are they created and are they part of the source?

Answer

The collective of low energies that affect human beings and make them go against their own growth can be seen as unpurified energy that exists close to Earth's atmospheres. This unpurified energy once existed in a physical body. At the end of a life cycle, all beings have to go through a process of purification. For some, this process is so complex that it cannot be completed and this energy still exists in the Earth's atmospheres and is not able to return to the astral plane. This energy can manipulate, pollute, and feed on human beings on Earth. They manipulate people's minds planting thoughts of fear, confusion, limitation or sometimes they appear as powerful light beings that have absolute control of life on Earth. If you have experienced this you have to understand and accept that these beings are part of Earth's distortion and as Earth is purifying from this you have to do the same.

When you have healed yourself and purified your whole being, connecting to the light then this distorted energy will have no power to enter your being.

Question

My questions have to do with the Bible. Who wrote the Bible and what was its initial purpose? Has it been mistranslated from the original meaning? Is it meant for truth or deception? It has been proven that the Bible has secret codes in its texts, and I read a scientific study that showed how human DNA is encoded with Bible verses. Is this true, and if so why? Also, a lot of the things on Earth are perceived as evil such as demons and people who choose to harm others. Is there a necessary purpose for this 'evil?'

Answer

All ancient teachings were written symbolically as well as literally and they all contain many layers of understanding and hidden esoteric knowledge. The bible is divided into two parts the Old Testament and the New Testament. The New Testament was a text which contained hidden occult knowledge but it was mainly used to establish Christianity as the new religion in the west. The religion of Christianity was already formed when the New Testament was written.

The Old Testament is a collection of historical and legendary facts and covers a period of thousands of years. If you are looking for truth, the Old Testament stands in a better place than the New Testament. However, the text of the Old Testament has been also misinterpreted, parts of it were lost and additions were made to promote the establishment of that time.

People on Earth understand the world around them as a polarity of good and evil. This is a characteristic of the third-dimensional perception. All beings are in a process of growing and evolving. Your path has challenges and you will be called to make decisions for your own life and focus on staying on your path. You can escape illusion, reclaim your power, connect to your astral body, and raise your vibration. Some people choose to give up their powers, others prefer to ignore their true-self and follow the growth of the blind and the deaf. When you choose this path you are harming yourself and you become a victim of your own ignorance.

Question

Everything being a probability, then there is an Earth where the golden age already happened, is in progress, and we can be that Earth, so what is it there to save? Isn't there the risk of people of Earth to become dependent on the gods? How do you take back your power from the governments?

Answer

There is free will and there is personal growth or stagnation. The whole creation is in constant evolution because our source is in constant evolution. We are all part of our creator and we all receive light from it. All beings have an individual and a cosmic purpose. People, who live on Earth right now, have a personal growth plan. If they follow their path and fulfill their purpose, they will have completed a cycle of evolution. All beings that are reincarnated, they connect to the Earth energies, and part of their purpose is to help the planet raise her vibration. On the other hand, Earth is also offering her light and nourishment to all her creation. The planet has also a growth plan and a purpose. So we are all supporting each other to grow, evolve, and get to a higher state.

We are all connected. We are receiving and transmitting light; this is one of the cosmic laws. Gods' purpose is to create, maintain the cosmic laws, and transmit high energy to the creation. We do not wish to be involved with the lives of beings. The reason we communicate with you right now is that you are trapped in a space of distortion and destruction and it is our duty to safeguard life in all panes. When you are evolved as a whole planet and you are free from the illusion we will have fulfilled our purpose and direct communication will not be necessary.

Your government does not have true power because their intention is not growth and evolution. You are convinced that you have to obey so without knowing you give your powers away. Stop believing in the illusion. Stop trying to achieve social success criteria. Know your true-self. Have empathy and genuine interest in others. Live a life of truth and growth. Do not focus on material instead concentrate on your purpose and the tools are given to you.

Question

Can you provide more information on different consciousnesses both on earth and beyond? Do other planets for instance have a similar problem with this parasitic type consciousness that is here on Earth?

Answer

Consciousness is not the distortion that people on Earth experience in their everyday life. It is not the illusion that spreads through their mind and the fear patterns. Consciousness highlights your ability to grow and everything that you carry in you that supports this growth. The distortion that affects the human mind is not the greatest force on Earth. There is high growth therefore high consciousnesses on Earth that are helping this planet to create life and expand her energy field. It seems that the consciousnesses of humanity are not identical to the consciousnesses of Earth.

This is why humanity should stop focusing on Illusionary and harmful ways of living and go back to Earth and be taught by her. The people who accept the importance of truly connecting to Earth and allow her to teach you how to grow on the planet will understand Earth's consciousness and this will become their consciousnesses. It is interesting that the people who are demonstrating, complaining, and spending a lot of their time trying to save Earth, they also exist in a maze of distortion and illusion. All these people have to stop arguing and create communities where they can truly connect to Earth and grow with her.

Question

What is the promised land?

Answer

Human beings are very attracted to the idea of the promised land, a location that can give them all resources they need so they can fulfil their dream of everlasting happiness. This promised land exists and it is in their being: connecting to their whole being, allowing the light to guide them to their path, develop their special abilities, fulfil their purpose and see themselves as receivers and transmitters of light.

If human beings were able to connect to the Earth and the cosmos they would be able to understand the purpose of this lifetime. They will be able to see that there is a path created for them to help them achieve their purpose effortlessly. Human beings who are suffering from distortion have no clarity therefore they cannot see their path and their connection with Earth and the cosmos. Instead, they follow diversions, taking them to illusionary states, hoping that they can create a wonderful life and fulfil their purpose there. Many people relocate to the big cities of your western civilisation.

They leave their towns and countries behind and enter the big cities in order to grab their own opportunities of success. Big cities were created to attract, control and manipulate a big number of people who are looking for a better life. It is important to know that everything that is created by the rulers focuses on control and to shut down people's true potential for growth. Technology, financial stability, opportunities of success and the many choices that are available to people in the cities are all a powerful force of destruction.

Currently, human beings are being affected by a health crisis that has shaped every aspect of their lives. The people who are suffering the most are the people in the big cities of your western civilisation and this was meant to be this way. The rulers are going to create more of these crisis events in the coming years and again the people in the cities will suffer the most because they are disconnected from Earth. If you wish to step out from the control you have to connect to Earth and allow her to nourish you.

Question

Lately I find that I must disassociate myself from people, because they are either toxic, or a distraction by numerous means, such as drama.

In some cases, these are family members, and I wonder how to balance family obligations with my need to focus on my own growth and well-being. It seems that there is an equal force that wants us to fail, and the more we work on ourselves, the more obstacles it seems one must overcome. Does Thoth have any words of advice?

Answer

People who are close to you need to be treated with kindness and understanding. Being on your path and trying to bring clarity in your life does not mean that you have to cut your ties with the people who are genuinely connected to you even if your understanding and perception of the cosmos is very different from theirs.

You can enjoy being with people that have a different path from you. What is important is that you both genuinely care for each other and you are willing to support each other with your light.

Trying to convince people about your understanding of life with words and opposition will make you both vulnerable and your light will not be shared so it will become weak. When you are able to see yourself as a free and pure being with unlimited opportunities you will be guided by your light. Your light will help you to connect to people around you and create meaningful relationships as well as experience a balanced life.

If you are experiencing obstacles on your way to growth this means that you have not yet met your true- self and you are still influenced by the illusion which is blocking your way. Challenge yourself; try to connect to your true-self away from all artificiality. This is your path and it is open.

Question

What does Thoth know about abortion? When does the soul enter the fetus? What are the consequences?

Answer

What you call abortion we understand as the end of live cycle or the inability for an undeveloped physical being to enter fully the physical reality. When this happens it seems to you that the parents decide to terminate this life cycle of an unborn baby. In reality the unborn baby is not ready to fulfil its purpose as a physical being and return back to the astral plane.

The essence, the light, of an astral being is responsible for the creation process of the body of an unborn baby. The soul is the connection between the physical body and the astral body. The process is not always the same and this depends on the light of the astral being, the light and physicality of the parents and the purpose of the newborn. There is a long preparation for this to happen and for every birth there is a cosmic purpose as well as an individual one.

Question

How do I know the difference between guidance from my higher self and the ego? I hear "intuition" often, but I have a hard time discerning if the first thing that comes to me is truly intuition of my ego telling me what I want to hear.

Answer

Human beings are affected by many voices and it happens that when you are strongly connected to illusion that the voice of your ego is the loudest. If you are looking for clarity you have to find your way to your true-self and this can be done by examining and testing all the information that comes to you. The voice of the ego often talks to you about survival, fear, negativity, short lived success which is often linked to competition and scheming. The voice of the ego will never tell you the truth about your current situation; you find yourself often looking at the pyramid trying to go up the steps and receive the illusionary prizes. If ego does not encourage you to go up the steps of the pyramid then it is going to terrorize you with the idea of suffering, fear and disability. The voice of ego will never bring you peace and only when you are in peace you are connected to truth. If you are in doubt try to enter a space of peace, see your body as a multidimensional being receiving and transmitting cosmic energy. Disconnect from your illusionary state to enter the cosmic state and then see yourself reincarnated on Earth to fulfil a unique purpose. In this state you will be able to connect to truth and the voice of the ego will fade away.

Question

My question has to do with the golden era: are there any parts of the Earth that are experiencing the golden era already; What will be the transformation and growth process for Earth in order to return to the golden era; how this will affect her creation including humanity; how can human beings support Earth's growth and transformation?

Answer

The Golden Era has not left Earth. Close to the core of the planet, Earth's essence, the golden era is still affecting Earth's light and tries to move to the surface and reunite the planet's whole being. In the areas close to the core, the golden era is transforming the life that exists there. The light of the golden era can reach the surface of the Earth in places where there are certain entrances that were used in the past as tunnels of communication between all parts of Earth. These are high vibrational areas and most of them are unknown to humanity. If you want to support Earth's transformation and the return of the golden era to the whole planet, you have to purify yourselves, receive light, become a pure receiver and transmitter of the cosmic light and allow it to spread on the surface of Earth. The light of the golden era that exists in the core of the Earth, it is the cosmic light and the source's creative force.

Question

What would help or benefit me to find inner stillness and peace again?

Answer

There are parts of you that have remained hidden and you can experience absolute peace when you connect to your whole being. See your being as a house of many rooms. Only when you are able to open all the doors, observe and experience all parts of your house then you will be able to use it effectively for a comfortable living and wellbeing. Do not be afraid to enter all the rooms and discover your special abilities, the truth and growth that you carry, the light that can help you transform becoming a perfect receiver and transmitter of cosmic light on Earth. When you know yourself you will enter a state of peace and you will start to grow.

Question

Is fasting good for your body?

Answer

Human's way of consuming food that is available to them is very problematic. People who are able to grow the food they eat, they truly nourish their being with food that is alive. This is a way to connect to Earth and receive her energy. When you start consuming alive fruit and vegetables your eating patterns will change. The combination of what you eat is also important as well as when you eat it. Most human beings are eating often but they feel constantly hungry. They do not realise that their food makes them tired and unsatisfied. Eating is a great way to connect to your being and understand its function and ways of growth. When you eat polluted food, you bring imbalance to your body that often leads to disease. Human beings should grow their own food and eat what they produce, connecting to Earth and bringing balance to their body. If you are not able to produce your own food at this moment, a step forward will be to pick the fruit and vegetables that are grown locally and have what you call "fasting". Limiting your food intake, preparing raw meals and juices should be your everyday diet. This will help you purify your body and also disconnect you from the need of consumption, the fear of survival and the greed that brings destruction to the planet. If you are able to fast for a few days you will experience a feeling of peace and you will be able to disconnect from artificiality and illusions. Your connection to your being will be stronger and the energies of Earth will be flowing in you and nourish you.

Question

Where are people's memories stored?

Answer

When you experience your life as a whole being, you will know that memories are energy patterns that can lead you to growth. Memories related to trauma; this is a process for you to purify yourself, to observe how events have affected your being but also to create a new healing space for yourself where you can find peace.

Memories can connect you to past events and remembering can help you see your life as a flow, a movement within your being whose true purpose is growth. When memories bring pain and unresolved issues, this means that your being is affected by distortion. Therefore your whole being including your perception of your actions and thoughts is distorted and fragmented.

Your memories can also become a tool for distortion to spread, injecting fear into your being. Being in a state of peace, accepting your path and purpose, purifying from all illusion and distortion are steps that can support your whole being to grow; this is when memories become a tool of growth. Your memories are energy patterns that are spread to your whole being. If you are able to expand towards the creative force of Earth and the cosmos, you are going to have memories of creation.

If this reincarnation is related to a previous one and you are open to receive the light of the cosmos, you will have memories from this previous lifetime. All creation is happening in the astral plane. This is a high plane where all life is created; the astral body is eternal and in constant growth supporting growth in many planes. If you are looking for a place where creation is taking place and cosmic memories are stored, this is the astral plane. All human beings have access to the astral plane through their astral body. Unity is a cosmic law that supports growth.

VOCABULARY

Astral body is an extension of your physical body and occupies a great area of energetic fields called the astral plane. The astral body is in constant growth, connecting to the high light of the cosmos and following the cosmic laws in order to receive and transmit the high light of the cosmos. Having a physical form does not restrict you from connecting to your astral body and becoming part of growth and evolution that takes place there. Connecting to your truth and purpose and going through the process of purification, transformation and growth, you are allowing constant connection and communication between your physical and astral body.

Astral plane is the true home of all beings. In the astral plane all physical beings lose their physicality and exist in their pure form which is their light.

The astral plane is a place of transformation and growth. It is the home of all beings; it is the home of all creation. Beings have their own purpose and their own plan for growth and this is why the astral plane is divided into many subplanes which have different frequency levels. Beings are not left on their own to seek truth and growth but they are connected to many other beings that have the same frequency as them; they connect to higher beings who are their guides and lower beings that are supported by them. In the astral plane there is no destruction, all beings have clarity and therefore they experience their plan of growth.

In this state you receive guidance from your higher-self and divine intervention from your creation code. Your astral body is aware of your purpose and growth cycles; cosmic truth and wisdom goes through the astral body in the form of energy and this is why it is in a process of constant purification and transformation.

Aura is an electromagnetic field that surrounds all physical bodies and allows them to receive and transmit energy. Your aura helps you communicate energetically, supports the body to function and stay balanced, staying grounded and connecting to the cosmos and astral body. Distortion and fragmentation can affect the aura as well as the physical body.

Code of Creation (creation code) is a "geometric" code which is used to create and maintain life. Our source is always within us; we all carry the creation code which is a living being and is affected by our consciousness, the light that we possess and the way we use it. The unity that exists in the cosmos is contained in the light of our creator and is spread to the creation through our creation code. The creation code can be understood as the intention of the source to create life. All beings are connected to the source because every part of their being in all planes is connected to the creation code. All beings that exist in all planes are created in the astral plane and therefore they have an astral body which is in constant transformation and growth. The guide of the astral body is the higher self. The higher self is aware of all transformation and growth, all connections, duties and paths that the astral body can experience. The higher self supports the astral body to follow the cosmic laws, experience unity with the cosmos, receive and transmit light and move closer to the source by supporting growth in all planes. The creation code is the high seed of all beings and it exists with the source. All beings are able to connect to the source to their creation code. The gods do not have access to the creation code but they do connect to the higher self. The creation code cannot be altered; the source creates through the gods using the cosmic light and then the gods become the source's creative tool.

Consciousness contains the "highlights" of one's growth and has two main uses: one is to record, maintain and stabilise one's growth and second is to be used as a guide for other entities who wish to work with this person in the astral or physical plane. There is also a collective consciousness which some people confuse with the beliefs of certain social groups. Collective is the consciousness of Earth and its reflection to all beings that live on the planet. This is when a unit of growth connects with other units of growth who are affected by the same electromagnetic fields.

Cosmic laws are a reflection of the natural laws which exist on Earth. All planes are regulated by cosmic laws. When these cosmic laws are not followed we have high levels of distortion and imbalances similarly to what Earth is experiencing right now. Enlightenment is the result of our connection and understanding of the cosmic laws. Everything we seek is waiting for us if we connect to the cosmos and act accordingly. Another cosmic law is the unity of all creation brings energy, balance, strength to receivers and transmitters and more opportunity for further growth.

Cosmic light is the light of our source which spreads to all creation. Its purpose is to offer life, growth and guidance and connect all creation. High creator gods have the ability to connect to the light of the creator to create life. Gods are not in control of this high creative force, they do not fully understand how it works and furthermore, they cannot reproduce it. Instead, the light creates through them. When the High Light passes information from the creation code, the form of a being first develops in the astral plane. In the physical plane, beings learn to experience life through the five senses or the limitations of a physical body. Beings that experience an astral existence simultaneously with their physical reality are able to acquire knowledge leading to a new cycle of growth.

Clarity is the clear understanding of one's purpose. Having clarity you are able to see your path and create all the necessary circumstances to help you achieve your goal. Clarity is a divine tool given to all beings to enable them to communicate with their astral body and connect them to their purpose. Clarity can be achieved if we simply look deep inside ourselves, connect to our purity, and make it our guide.

Distortion is an energetic imbalance that has affected Earth and her creation and is caused by the trauma of Earth, the end of her golden era and her disability to cope as a high creator. The third dimensional reality, with its lower vibration, is the ideal space for distortion to grow and expand. As a result people live in a constant hypnotic state of illusion and stagnation disconnected from the purpose and divine plan.

Duality is the separation of self from all that exists. When children start to become aware of society structures, they start to lose their ability to experience unity. The focus in their lives will be indoctrination, focusing on the mind-logic-limitation and being part of a life of duality, fragmentation and non-growth. There is always a fight of the opposites which is the cause of fragmentation and illusion. If you wish to evolve beyond duality, you have to disconnect from the idea of opposites. In nature there is no fight against two elements there is only a union of the elements, bringing new life.

Enlightenment is not our final destination in our quest for growth but is just a single step towards gnosis. Masters have to take many steps of enlightenment in order to comprehend just a small piece of the vastness of cosmos. Becoming receivers and transmitters of light, you allow the cosmic flow to enter humanity and Earth.

Essence is the presence of the High Source which nobody can destroy or alter. Our growth depends on our ability to create and for this to happen we have to recognize and understand our essence and our creation code. The essence of Earth, in the physical plane, can be described as the golden era, a time of high creation.

Fragmentation is an imbalance on Earth that can be understood as a separation of self from all that exists. On Earth, beings experience fragmentation that affects inner unity, clarity and disability to connect to your purpose and truth. Fragmentation can affect the connection between humanity and Earth and allow the cosmic light to be received and transmitted to all life.

Gnosis is wisdom.

The Golden Era was a time of high creation. In the golden era, all beings had a different cycle. Their light was eternal and they were able to be reborn. The colours and the shapes on Earth gave her a high vibration and all creation was connected to this. The cosmic laws ruled Earth's existence and purity was clearly seen and experienced in all beings. Everything that existed on Earth had to produce light and energy to support the planet's growth. The whole planet was united and went through purification and transformation as a whole being. They received light from the high realms and they transmitted light to support the cosmos. In the golden era, there were many beings that were able to nourish themselves with the light. The animal kingdom received nourishment directly from the Earth and other beings on the planet were connected to the light of the cosmos. What you are experiencing in your time, animals eating each other, started to take place when the vibration of Earth became lower. During the golden era, Earth resembled what you now call exotic and tropical nature. Earth was created to have enough resources to feed and nourish all her creation. Plants and animals were fed with the minerals and other nutrients which could be found on Earth as well as the light from the electromagnetic fields of the planet.

Growth is synonymous to life. All living beings have multiple opportunities to transform and grow, receiving and transmitting the cosmic light. All of you come on Earth to fulfil your purpose, this means to achieve growth and spread this growth to humanity and Earth. You will be given opportunities to achieve this and the events are recorded in your divine plan. There are people who are going to pollute their being with artificiality and distortion; this is their choice. They are responsible for their own growth and when they go against their growth, their opportunities diminish.There is a divine plan that shapes a being's existence but human beings with their actions, thoughts and creation can increase or decrease their opportunities of growth.

Higher-self is the true essence of a being and exists in a much higher vibration than the astral body. The higher-self directed evolution and connects to the astral body when certain light and information is needed for its growth. Everything that exists is really a reflection of a lower or a higher related body. In other words all bodies are reflections of each other.

High Creator has no form, character or attributes. Our High Creator is the perfect representation of life where everything is effortless, whole and limitless. High Gods can only dream to be in this state of absolute perfection, where there is nothing to see and yet everything exists simultaneously. Our High Creator is not a human being; it is a state of the highest growth and the highest consciousness. Our Creator is limitless: its whole creation, everything that exists, it is only a fragment of our source's existence.

Illusion appears as multiple layers of distorted reality that people accept as true. It is highly versatile and being formless can take any temporary form. When human beings receive this temporary form of illusion and accept it as real, they give it life and form which is able to grow and implant on different people. Illusion does not have a form or growth and has the tendency to connect to low-self; it becomes part of this person's experience and then quickly needs to spread to others in order to acquire power.

Logos is a vibrational creation tool, pure reflection of our source, which is given to high gods to create life. Logos is a communication between source and the living being high god and through this connection the creative intention of the source goes through the lower being who is the creator god and through him/her the source creates.

New Planes consist of multiple subplanes and were created as an extension of the astral plane. The new planes became the home of physical creation and went through many transformations to support physical creation and the overall growth and balance. The new planes were also called lower planes because of the low vibration, distortion and imbalances that affected the physical creation.

Pleroma is a separate plane which exists in direct connection with the source. The Pleroma is the highest plane and consists of different energetic layers and subdivisions. It is inhabited by gods and god creators.

Polarity is a division that creates two opposites. This is an imbalance that can be experienced in low vibrational states where the human mind distracts the natural and cosmic processes of a being. Polarity goes against unity and creates obstacles for people to accept, remain in peace or connect to the truth in them.

Purification is a process of cleansing all imbalances, blockages, fears, limitations, and restrictions of illusionary patterns/beliefs/state in order to experience your true abilities, weaknesses, strengths, talents and skills. The process of purification includes observation, practice of self-love and acceptance, creating a space of peace, connecting to Earth and the cosmos and allowing truth to guide you to your path.

Purity is this part of you that cannot be affected by any sort of manipulation, fragmentation and distortion. All beings carry purity in them. It is their light, which was given to them when they were created. It is the link between the being, the god and the source. When you follow purity, you are truly happy and satisfied; able to make your greatest contribution in your life and in the life of others; transform yourself and others; have no doubt as to what your purpose is and you will be able to fulfil it.

Purpose of a being is related to the divine plan and the true expression of life. Third-dimensional beings can fulfil their purpose and can experience growth if they are able to clear blockages and imbalances.

Reincarnation offers the opportunity to a being to receive and offer teachings. People reincarnate wherever and whenever there is a need for this to happen. They are beings who have reincarnated many times on Earth and they are other beings who have reincarnated on many others planets, galaxies and universes. For every being there is a divine plan, a plan of evolution, and this is stored in its creation code and is manifested on its higher-self. According to this plan, beings will go through a certain learning process that is tailored specifically for them.

Schism is a severe form of fragmentation that can create strong polarities, imbalances and destruction. Earth's inability to heal herself and her creation led to complete detachment from gods' intervention. When human beings create great schisms in them, they can lose their humanity; they become a different species.

Soul is a great educator and guides beings to their true purpose. It is an aid, helping beings to open up to their astral existence and what lies beyond that. In the beginning of a reincarnation, a link is created between the physical and the astral body and when the body dies this link, which is the soul, disconnects from the physical body and goes back to the astral. Soul does not evolve and it is not the purest part of a being as many think.

Transformation is a process of rebirth. When you are in transformation you are able to produce, transmit and receive different energies and use your light to achieve great growth.

True-self helps us understand our purpose and our tools. It is important that you safeguard your truth and do not let others pull you into the illusion with their criticism and negativity. Let your light guide you and others; enjoy a balanced life unknown to many and bring this gift to others. People who follow truth have an effortless life because they are balanced and exist to fulfil their purpose. People who are aware of their true-self have nothing to hide and their evolution and growth are guaranteed.

Wormholes and stargates are entrance points on Earth. There are different types of star gates, some of them are divine creation and others were built by beings from other planets who wish to visit Earth. The star gates created by the gods are placed on important points of the Earth's grid and this corresponds to the star gates on different planets and galaxies. These entrances form an energetic shape which works as a magnet for constant energy flow and balance. The star gates which were created by beings can be found in secret locations in the physical plane as well as in different planes which mirror the physical Earth. These star gates connect different geographical points on Earth as well as places on other planets and other dimensions.

Life is growth and this is experienced in all planes. Earth will tell you this when you are able to connect to her and will show you that birth never stops and has no end. This is how you should see your lives; constantly growing, transforming, becoming the womb for the cosmic light to create and then experience growth around you. If you ignore this cosmic law then you exist in illusion and you are responsible for blocking your own growth and connection to the Source.

NOTES

NOTES

NOTES

NOTES

NOTES